Advance Praise

"Frontline sales managers are the most important lever for leading change in a sales organization—yet most companies still don't adequately prepare them. In *The Sales Managers Guide to Greatness,* Kevin Davis provides practical, actionable, and proven-effective content to help you prepare and enable your sales managers to be the proactive, productive leaders and sales coaches they need to be, to get the results you want from your sales force."

—**Mike Kunkle**, Senior Director of
Sales Readiness Consulting, Brainshark

"*The Sales Manager's Guide to Greatness* provides a powerful message for any leader whose success is determined by their team's sales performance. We've measured not only an improvement in our sales managers' skills but, more importantly, a positive impact on our sales force and bottom-line results."

—**Jim Ferguson**,
VP of Sales, Holland Transportation

"This fast-moving, practical book shows you how to immediately boost the performance and productivity of every salesperson. It will make you look like a genius!"

—**Brian Tracy**, Author,
The Psychology of Selling

"Everyone knows that the effectiveness of a sales manager is the biggest factor determining a team's success. In *The Sales Manager's Guide To Greatness*, Kevin Davis describes 10 practical strategies that sales managers can use to elevate their own game—and create a champion team."

—**Mark O'Leary**, VP of Enterprise,
Western Division, Comcast Business

"We all accept—at least I hope we do—that the sales management function in every company is now pivotal to the overall success of the organization. The sales team is the offense and if they are not scoring consistently then the team has a very bleak future. However, in order to maintain optimum performance levels the team needs a strong leader and coach. Therein lies the challenge, because we believe that 80% of managers lack that capability. *The Sales Manager's Guide to Greatness* provides a superb route map, which is easy to follow and implement. This is not a book to be read just once and put on the bookshelf; rather, it is genuinely a guide which should be referred to daily until the skills are fully adopted."

—**Jonathan Farrington**,
CEO, Top Sales World;
Executive Editor, *Top Sales Magazine*

"If your sales force isn't producing the results you need them to, it isn't likely that it's because they are poor performers. It's more likely that they need to be better led. The coaching section in *The Sales Manager's Guide to Greatness* alone will help you remedy this problem—and faster than you'd believe. Read it now, and implement it immediately."

—**Anthony Iannarino**, Author,
The Only Sales Guide You'll Ever Need

"*The Sales Manager's Guide to Greatness* debunks the myths surrounding what it takes to be a great sales manager once and for all and offers clear solutions and takeaways. This is more than a book—it's your map to success."

—**Mark Hunter**, author of *High-Profit Prospecting*

"*The Sales Manager's Guide to Greatness* fills the much-needed gap of developing sales management skills. This is a comprehensive, pragmatic guide for putting sales leaders and leadership into action with results."

—**Louis Carter**, Author,
Best Practices in Talent Management
and *The Change Champion's Field Guide*

"I'm always excited about books that help managers become true leaders—and *The Sales Manager's Guide to Greatness* is one of those books. In it, Kevin Davis describes the full range of skills and mindsets needed to be an effective leader and coach. Read this book and learn how to lead your team to the top!"

—**Ken Blanchard**, Coauthor,
The New One Minute Manager® and
Collaboration Begins with You

"This really is an excellent piece of work. I like very much the way Kevin has created a one-step-at-a-time plan, guiding both novice and experienced sales managers alike through a program of self-improvement. This ensures that managers are not overwhelmed by attempting to implement too much, too quickly. This should be a must-read for all managers who have an ambition to develop into genuine leaders."

—**Linda Richardson**, Founder of Richardson;
Best-selling Author; Consultant;
Faculty, Wharton Graduate School

The Sales Manager's Guide to Greatness

10 Essential Strategies for
Leading Your Team to the Top

Kevin F. Davis

GREENLEAF
BOOK GROUP PRESS

Published by Greenleaf Book Group Press
Austin, Texas
www.gbgpress.com

Copyright ©2017 Kevin F. Davis

Distributed by Greenleaf Book Group

For ordering information or special discounts for bulk purchases, please contact Greenleaf Book Group at PO Box 91869, Austin, TX 78709, 512.891.6100.

Design and composition by Greenleaf Book Group
Cover design by Greenleaf Book Group

Image Copyright bizvector and Alex Gontar, 2016.
Used under license from Shutterstock.com
Author photo by Ciprian Photography

Cataloging-in-Publication data is available.

Print ISBN: 978-1-62634-388-7
eBook ISBN: 978-1-62634-389-4
Audiobook ISBN: 978-1-62634-423-5

Part of the Tree Neutral® program, which offsets the number of trees consumed in the production and printing of this book by taking proactive steps, such as planting trees in direct proportion to the number of trees used: www.treeneutral.com

TreeNeutral®

Printed in the United States of America on acid-free paper

17 18 19 20 21 22   10 9 8 7 6 5 4 3 2 1

First Edition

Dedicated to my two Emmas, one here and one there.

Before you are a leader,

success is all about growing yourself.

When you become a leader,

success is all about growing others.

—Jack Welch

Acknowledgments

Much gratitude to our clients and their sales managers who participated in our two-day sales management workshops. Many of the ideas and examples in this book grew out of the opportunities provided to us by our valued clients.

Thanks to Sue Reynard, editor par excellence. The person behind the scenes who makes my work look better in so many ways.

Thanks to Tom Gundrum, TopLine Leadership's director of training, for his tireless dedication to our clients for more than two decades. Tom made important contributions to the development of the C.O.A.C.H. Model.

Thanks to trusted advisors Christian Maurer and Bob Beckerman, both of whom have sharpened my thinking.

Patrick Conte provided many invaluable insights related to "a day in the life" from his EVP of Sales perspective.

Thanks to David Roache whose thoughtful suggestions helped shape the final manuscript.

The name "Willie Sellmore" was created by humorist Jack Fiala.

Thank you to my wife, Dale, for putting up with me for the past 35 years. Simply put, I couldn't have done it without you.

Introduction

Every sales manager's job is to drive consistent sales growth. That means maximizing their team's performance. But from what I see, many sales managers aren't going about meeting this challenge in the most effective way. Let me explain.

A few years ago, a major office equipment company conducted a survey of its 1,500 business-to-business salespeople, asking them to rate how well their sales managers did in 80 categories. Here are the skills that the sales managers ranked the best and worst at:

- **Best** (#1 of 80): Wants me to succeed

- **Worst** (#80 of 80): Views one of their priorities as developing my individual skills

As you can see, sales managers at this company *wanted* their salespeople to be successful but were dead last in providing the hands-on sales coaching and teaching that salespeople needed to actually get better.

This pattern is all too familiar to me. I talked recently with a young sales manager, Nick, who'd only been managing for about 18 months after spending a number of years as a sales rep. Nick told me that at first he loved the 14-hour days, loved interacting with salespeople and being seen as the go-to person for advice, and loved getting involved in all of the big deals. Lately, though, he confessed, "I feel like I'm holding on for dear life, overwhelmed by an avalanche of stuff to do."

Then he added, "Between hiring the new rep last year, trying to keep track of everyone's numbers, and dealing with the barrage of emails and calls and meeting requests I get every single day—it just feels overwhelming. I'd like to spend more time with each rep, but that just isn't possible."

I work all the time with sales managers like Nick who want their people to succeed (like the #1 item on the survey). Almost all were hired (or more likely promoted) into the position so they could share their talents, skills, and positive attitude with their salespeople. But somewhere along the way, that "avalanche of stuff" overwhelms them: fires to fight, meetings to attend, voice mails and emails to answer. So they don't get around to doing much teaching or coaching (item #80 on the survey). That's why so many sales managers need a way to conquer the "stuff," to become more strategic in the use of their time and coaching investment, and to find more effective ways to optimize their team. That is the best path toward maximizing sales results.

Closing the gap between the intent of wanting people to succeed and actions needed to *actually* accomplish that is the goal of *The Sales Manager's Guide to Greatness*.

The Impact of Effective Sales Coaching

I can empathize with all of the Nicks out there. Many organizations do a lot to prepare their salespeople to *sell* but very little to prepare their sales managers to *lead and manage* a sales team. They regularly invest in sales training and provide reps with a wide variety of resources on how to do their jobs (books, seminars, methodologies, tools). Yet sales managers get just a fraction of the training investment that their teams do. As a consequence, they know how to sell but often don't know how to make their sales teams great.

The disparity between how much companies invest in their sales-people vs. their sales managers doesn't make sense to me. It's simple math: Improve *one* sales manager's skills and you improve an *entire team's* performance and results. This isn't just my opinion. A research report from the Sales Management Association (SMA) published in late 2015[1] concluded that **coaching improvement is high-yield**. The firms included in the research that were able to help their managers deliver high-quality coaching to salespeople **realized annual revenue growth nearly 17 percent higher** than those that did not do any coaching development for managers.

The SMA report also confirms that effective sales coaching is a matter of both time (quantity) and quality. Overall, **less than 8 percent** of a sales manager's workload in the studied firms was allocated to coaching. Moreover, we have to question how that 8 percent is being used. While sales managers often tell me they are doing a lot of "coaching," when I ask them to describe what they do, it turns out they are only reviewing past performance (the numbers) and activity, and discussing impending deals. That kind of activity is what I label **performance management**.

This kind of review of outcomes is an important aspect of managing a sales team. But to have a team that continually improves, you also need to do **developmental coaching**, work that helps your reps improve their sales skills and mental attitude.

One of the most effective ways I've found to illustrate the difference between performance management and developmental coaching is this:

> When you play golf, you write your score for each hole
> on the scorecard. At the end of the round, the scorecard
> will tell you which holes you did well on and which

---

1   "Research Brief: Support Sales Coaching," The Sales Management Association (November, 2015).

ones you didn't. But the scorecard doesn't tell you why. Your performance was not determined by the number you wrote down for how many strokes you made. Your score was the result of the good and bad swings (and decisions) you made while playing.

If you gave a golf coach your scorecard and asked them to get you back on track, they can't really help you. All they can see is the aftermath of what you did and offer their assessment based on incomplete information.

To help you improve, your golf coach would need to observe you and work with you to set improvement goals, identify gaps in your skills, and create a plan for filling those gaps. That's developmental coaching. That approach increases the odds that changes and improvements will happen. All of us are more motivated to implement advice when it is specific and thoughtful.

The scorecard metaphor is directly applicable to sales performance management where sales managers such as Nick review individual reps' activity levels and sales results and then offer their assessments accordingly. I'm not disparaging performance management. Salespeople need regular feedback from managers on how they are doing; they need to know that they are being held accountable for fulfilling their job responsibilities.

But for far too many sales managers who are overwhelmed like Nick, performance management is the only form of feedback they have time to provide. That means sales teams suffer from a lack of developmental coaching advice; reps never get to learn the lessons that experienced former reps like Nick could teach them.

It's time to swing the pendulum more toward developmental coaching. A great sales coach is one who combines performance management with the necessary commitment to observe and teach that is so crucial to helping salespeople get better.

The purpose of this book is to provide you with a plan and methodology for doing exactly that so you can realize the kinds of growth rates that the high-coaching-level companies in the SMA survey saw.

What's in This Book

One of the clearest lessons I've learned in the past 20 years is that getting sales managers to coach more effectively is not simply a matter of teaching them coaching skills. They also need practical solutions to handle the barriers that *prevent* them from doing more coaching in the first place. That's why the book starts with two sections that address common factors that limit coaching time and effectiveness; they are followed by a section that covers coaching directly. Each section has an introduction that sets up the individual chapters; here is a quick overview of the theme of each section.

Section 1: Self-Leadership

In the discussions I've had with a multitude of sales VPs and directors, the single biggest frustration that I've heard over and over again is, "We promoted our top salesperson to sales manager, and it didn't work out like we thought it would." By which they mean that the sales manager was not able to achieve what the company wanted, which was to consistently exceed team quota, increase the number of reps on the team at or above plan (a.k.a. "team health"), and reduce sales rep turnover.

The two chapters in this section discuss the fundamental leadership mindsets that are characteristic of people who have made the mental transition from successful salesperson to great sales manager.

Section 2: Elements of Excellence

Many factors go into determining how well a sales team performs. This section talks about three of the most important elements that create a solid foundation for breakthrough performance: improving accountability for higher standards, getting the right people on the team, and teaching reps how to better match their *selling* to customer *buying*.

Section 3: Coach and Develop Your Team

Without the mindset and skills represented in the first two sections, sales managers won't have the appropriate priorities or focus when it comes to coaching their teams. Where those priorities should be placed is the subject of the four chapters in this section, which discuss developmental coaching and sales performance management from different perspectives.

Section 4: Taking Action

Sales managers who create great sales teams think about how to increase sales **not just for this quarter but over the long-term**. They know how to transform a sales team from where it is now to where it needs to be to meet those much higher quotas 6, 9, or 12 months from now. Great sales managers know how to move the needle quickly on the two most critical metrics: number of opportunities and win rates. There is just one chapter in this section, which talks about how to select your priorities and develop action plans.

Rising to the Challenge

Several years into my career as a sales rep in the office equipment business, my boss's boss, Mr. Kieran May, informed me he wanted to go on a field ride—spend a day working with me on sales calls. I was 27 at the time, making more money than I had ever imagined I could. I had independence and was loving life.

After the day working, we went out for a beer. Midway through the evening's conversation, Mr. May leaned toward me and said, "Kevin, congrats on your sales success. I have a question for you . . . do you plan to be a salesman for the rest of your life?"

He went on to say, "Anybody can learn how to sell. That's easy. But a much larger question is, *can you hire a team of salespeople and teach them how to sell like you do?* Kevin, I believe you have within you the ability to do great things. Will you decide to rise to this challenge?"

Looking back, I can say that learning to be an effective sales manager has definitely been a challenge, one made all the more difficult because of the lack of resources available at the time. My goal is to help all of the Nicks out there—all the sales managers who are now in the position I was once in. *The Sales Manager's Guide to Greatness* will help you think more strategically about your job, better manage your time and priorities so you can do more coaching and skill development for your team, and make sure you are getting maximum value out of every coaching conversation you have.

Section 1

Self-Leadership

Overview

By coincidence, just as I was finishing this book, I reconnected with an old client via LinkedIn. It was a sales manager I'd first trained 20 years ago. In the course of our exchanged messages, he mentioned there was one thing I'd told him back then that had really stuck with him: the need for sales managers to take ownership of everything that happens on a team, good *and bad*. "I learned that if I have the mental attitude that a problem is 'out there,' then *that's* the real problem," he recalled. "I always have to think about what I can do to make a situation better."

There was a double coincidence associated with this exchange because I'd just read a book called *Extreme Ownership*[2] about leadership in the Navy SEALs. The book was written by Leif Babin and Jocko Willink, two combat-proven US Navy SEAL officers who led the most highly decorated special operations unit of the Iraq War. (One of the soldiers on Babin and Willink's team was Chris Kyle, author of *The New York Times* best-seller *American Sniper*, which was the inspiration for the movie of the same name.)

Given what I'd been teaching for the past two decades, it was natural that I'd see connections between sales management and how SEALs train and prepare their leaders, mold and develop teams, and lead in combat.

---

2   Leif Babin and Jocko Willink, *Extreme Ownership: How U.S. Navy SEALs Lead and Win* (St. Martin's Press, 2015).

The authors point out that most leaders have a mindset that they are doing everything right. So when things go wrong, instead of looking at themselves, they blame others.

I've seen this a lot with sales managers. Suppose a team misses quota. The manager thinks they're doing everything right, so their only option is to lay the blame on things that others are doing unsatisfactorily: sales reps have too many cold or unqualified leads; marketing isn't asking the right questions; there's not enough technical staff to support trials; the new product hasn't been adequately tested. Whatever. These sales managers are thinking to themselves, "Well, I'm just going to do the best I can with what I have. A lot of these problems are out of my control."

Unfortunately, this attitude bleeds over to the sales rep. They have a problem and what do they say? "A lot of these problems are out of my control."

The exchange with my old acquaintance and the lessons from *Extreme Ownership* reminded me that the most important factor for success is the mentality of the sales manager leading a team. If that person thinks the problem is "out there," sustained success and continued improvement will be very hard to come by. But if the sales manager has the mindset of a leader and is committed to doing everything possible to help their team achieve what matters most, then anything is possible.

The chapters in this section of the book are devoted to helping you understand what it means to be the *leader* of a sales team, not just its *manager*.

Chapter 1: Embrace a Leadership Mindset discusses how to identify sales instincts that may be holding you back as a manager and how to replace them with more powerful leadership mindsets. Whether trained or untrained, novice or experienced, all sales managers run the risk of falling back on old habits and acting more like a super-salesperson than a leader.

Chapter 2: Take Control of Your Time and Priorities addresses what is, without question, the single most common complaint I hear from sales managers: They "don't have time" to coach. This chapter provides practical ideas for how sales managers can identify and focus on their priorities, including suggestions for how to act on the classic advice to separate the merely urgent from the truly important.

Chapter 1
Embrace a Leadership Mindset

I have two lists of attributes to show you:

List 1

- Speaks clearly and fluently

- Shows confidence in their abilities and ideas

- Provides value on a sales call

- Understands the needs of customers

List 2

- Assigns accounts fairly and equitably

- Ensures that new personnel receive the training and support they need

- Works with reporting employees to create a plan for their development

- Deals effectively with employees who do not meet their commitments

What's your impression of the difference between these lists? People usually tell me that List 1 sounds like the characteristics of a top sales performer while the items in List 2 are the things that good sales managers should be doing. Do you agree?

Here's the twist: Both lists include items from the survey I mentioned in the Introduction (p. 1) of 1,500 business-to-business salespeople who were asked to rate their managers on 80 categories. List 1 contains the items that filled out the rest of the top 5 things that salespeople think their managers do really well. List 2 is the rest of the bottom 5 items, meaning the things these managers did very poorly. Notice the pattern? According to salespeople, sales managers have great selling skills and not so great management skills.

These results confirm an observation I made many years ago: Sales managers find it too easy to fall back into their comfort zone, doing what they are already good at—namely, selling—and have a hard time making the switch to managing a sales team.

Why does this occur? Almost every sales manager I know was, at one point in their career, a peak-performing sales professional, the top dog on the team. Their organization then recognized their contributions and promoted them into a sales management role—and everything changed. Everything except perhaps them.

This presents a problem. Why? **Because managing and leading a sales team requires a completely different mindset from selling.** Yet what sales managers have to rely on are the instincts and competencies they developed when they were selling. Those instincts are part of their DNA; they stick around regardless of how long a former sales rep has been in a manager's role, whether 1 year, 10 years, or 20 years. With the dozens of decisions that sales managers face every day, they have no option but to go with what feels right in the moment, and for the most part what "feels right" will be informed by their sales instincts.

Overcoming these instincts is difficult for successful-reps-turned-managers. It simply doesn't occur to them that they will need to change something that has made them successful. Noted leadership consultant Ram Charan and his colleagues discuss this concept in their book *The Leadership Pipeline*: "The highest-performing people, especially, are reluctant to change; they want to keep doing the activities that made them successful."[3] And thus we learn that Sun Tzu was right when he said, "Eventually your strengths will become a weakness."

That's why, beyond any specific techniques you learn, you need to re-frame your thinking around a leadership mindset. Your decisions can't be based on what "feels right" from a salesperson's perspective; they have to be driven by what's good for your team. So challenge yourself with this question: *Are the competencies that made me a top salesperson inhibiting my effectiveness as a sales team leader?*

The answer is always yes. The odds are high that you are constantly fighting a subconscious war of instincts. (See sidebar, p. 18) Many times each day you are confronted by various issues and challenges. From what mindset—the salesperson or the sales team leader—are you making your daily decisions? Most of us just do what we instinctively feel is right.

Let's examine several ways in which this struggle plays out every day. I'll explain how some of the instincts possessed by great salespeople are the polar opposite of the mindset needed to become a more effective leader of a great sales team.

---

3 Ram Charan, Steve Drotter, and Jim Noel, *The Leadership Pipeline* (San Francisco, Jossey-Bass Inc., 2001), 17.

An example of instinct vs. leadership mindset struggles

When my son, Kyle, was seven years old, he signed up to play Little League baseball. His first year was difficult because he was unskilled. So I worked with him in the off-season to improve his throwing, hitting, and catching. In his second season, I volunteered to be assistant coach on his team. When the team met for the initial practices, I was sure that Kyle was at least the third-best player on the team. Yet when the team's season began, the head coach had Kyle batting last in the line-up and playing out in right field. (In Little League, right field is where you place your weakest player—something I know because I played right field when I was Kyle's age!)

Midway through the season, the head coach called and asked me to manage the team for the next game because he was sick. Naturally, I moved Kyle to second base and batted him leadoff. Were my instincts correct? Kyle struck out in every at bat and made five errors. I'll never forget watching my son boot another ground ball while listening to the parents complain about the new second baseman.

This isn't a story of Kyle's skill (or lack thereof). Kyle's performance that fateful day proved to me that, in my subconscious, I had been assessing Kyle from my instincts as a father rather than as a coach interested in having the whole team succeed. The same kind of struggle between what comes naturally and what is best for the team plagues sales managers every day.

War #1: Player vs. Observer

Every great salesperson I've known wanted to be in on the action, down on the field, making the plays. That strong drive is what made them great and brought them stellar results.

But sales managers are not put in the job to keep selling. They are put in the job so they can help *others* become the best salespeople they can be. Great sales managers see themselves as **observers** and **coaches**, not players.

Based on my own experience as a salesperson and manager and my observations (as a consultant) of sales managers over the past two decades, I can state unequivocally that this switch from player (sales rep) to observer (sales manager) is the hardest change all sales managers face. It takes a strong will to keep yourself from doing what you know you do better than everyone else on your team, and even the most experienced sales managers are prone to backslide to their sales instincts if they aren't vigilant.

My first year in sales, many years ago, I was awkward—and a slow learner. (Remember, I was a right fielder!) But my first sales manager, Guy Campbell, must have seen some potential because he invested a lot of time in coaching me. When Guy joined me on a customer meeting, I noticed he had a habit of pulling out a coin and placing it in the palm of his hand.

I didn't think anything of it until about three years later when I was promoted to sales manager in another office. Soon after, I ran into Guy at a corporate meeting and asked him why he always put a coin in his hand when he was out in the field with me. He responded, "Well, Kevin, when you were starting out, you were not very good. But I knew that in order for you to learn and improve I needed to keep my mouth shut. I couldn't jump in and take over every time you got in trouble. The only way I could keep silent was to squeeze that coin. The worse and worse you did, the harder and harder I squeezed. I needed to create a point of personal pain that was greater than the pain I felt watching you screw up a meeting!"

I've carried Guy's wisdom with me for many years and, mentally at least, squeezed a lot of coins in my day. And while I'm doing that squeezing, I'm taking note of the issues I want to talk over with the sales rep *after* the meeting. It's only by observing that I can properly evaluate what the problem is and offer suggestions that will lead to lasting improvements.

War #2: Closing vs. Coaching

What really catches the attention of a top sales rep is the opportunity for a big sale. Nothing gets our blood up like the chase! But that instinct for the chase and closing deals can lead us awry once we're in management.

Here's an example: A client of mine, Jackie, spent years developing into a stellar sales rep for her employer, a tech company. She had a well-earned reputation for producing results far beyond expectations. They duly rewarded her hard work by promoting her to the position of sales manager. Jackie later told me she was working harder than ever before—and yet her team's results were mediocre at best.

When Jackie was a sales rep, she was keenly focused on closing deals and getting results. As a sales manager, that instinct caused her to pay the most attention to her reps when their deals approached the close. It is what I call the "super-closer" syndrome.

I don't want to sound too critical of Jackie. As I've just discussed, it's natural to rely on the skills that got you somewhere in the first place, especially when, like Jackie, you were very good at what you did. But she had gotten into the habit of inserting herself into the sales process any time a big opportunity was on the horizon, barging in as if to say "move over, Rover, let the great one take over." Or she would turn her attention to a rep who was way under quota, swooping in at the last minute to try to help them close deals.

Neither of these approaches represents the best use of Jackie's time. The biggest deals are likely coming from her most experienced, highest-producing sales reps. While she's helping them do something they can likely do on their own, everyone else on the team is left to flounder. If she's focused on rescuing struggling reps, she's saving opportunities that probably aren't that great (if the rep had done a good job of identifying needs, the deal might not be in trouble in the first place—and if the customer doesn't think they have big needs, they won't agree to a big deal). Plus, the rep doesn't learn anything that will help them avoid a crisis the next time around. In both cases, the rest of the team has to struggle through on their own.

In her previous life as a rep, the biggest value Jackie provided to her company was closing sales. But that was no longer the case once she became a manager. My task was to help her see that **the biggest value she can provide her company now is to make sure her team continues to improve**.

The most important aspect of this change in mindset is learning to insert yourself earlier in the sales cycle to provide more effective coaching when it will do most the most good. If you look at an opportunity from the customer's perspective, a deal's size is largely determined very early on in the sales process, when the customer is recognizing the extent of their needs and determining their buying requirements. When Jackie coaches her sales reps in the early stage of a deal, she can help them ensure that the customer recognizes big, urgent needs and that their buying requirements are slanted in her company's favor. This kind of early-sales-cycle intervention will have the biggest impact on sales reps' results in both the short- and long-term.

Switching her focus from "being in on the close" to "coaching reps early on" will have many benefits for Jackie. For one thing, if a sales rep makes a mistake, Jackie will recognize it sooner, while there is still time to put the deal back on track. Ultimately, she'll start to see an increase in better qualified deals in her team's pipeline. When Jackie sees her team's results start to improve, she'll know that she has won this particular war with herself.

War #3: Tasks vs. People

Effective salespeople are high energy. They like to do stuff; they like to complete tasks. That drive contributes to their success as salespeople. "Getting things done" sounds like a good attribute for a sales manager, too, doesn't it?

Not so fast. A sales manager who is overly task oriented can spend too much time making sure mundane to-do items get done while ignoring the development needs of their salespeople.

This point came home to me when I read a story about Beth Comstock, once the chief marketing officer for General Electric and, as of 2016, a vice chair with the company. Comstock had started her career at NBC where everything was deadline driven—get it done by the six o'clock news. She admits to being very task oriented and wrote on LinkedIn[4] about an incident not long after she started at General Electric. She was in the middle of a phone conversation with her then-boss, Jack Welch, one of the most famous and influential CEOs of his day. Suddenly, the line went dead. She called Welch's assistant and said she and Jack had been disconnected. The assistant told Comstock that Jack had hung up on her. "He wants you to know that's what it's like to be in a meeting with you," the assistant said.

Welch later called Comstock into his office and told her she was "too efficient." Comstock's drive to complete her task list made her come across to others as "cold and abrupt." Welch told her that she needed to take more time to get to know her people and what is important to them.

Comstock says she heard, "loud and clear," the lesson that Jack Welch was teaching her and that, years later, she is still working on

---

4   Beth Comstock, "Best Advice: What I Learned from Jack Welch Hanging Up on Me," LinkedIn, February 26, 2013, https://www.linkedin.com/pulse/20130226113021-19748378-best-advice-what-i-learned-from-jack-welch-hanging-up-on-me

implementing that lesson. She has to continually remind herself that paying attention to people is a priority and that she needs to become more people-oriented and less task-driven.

Sales management is a contact sport. It's about spending time to get to know the strengths and weaknesses of each salesperson, about the relationships you develop with them. It's about knowing what you can do to get the most out of each rep. So, instead of focusing only on completing tasks, focus on your people. That means filling your time with coaching and helping your reps create their personal development plans. It means figuring out what motivates and demotivates each of your reps. It means making sure your team has the training and support they need to continually get better.

War #4: Results vs. Inputs

The sales profession is results-oriented. Every month you and your salespeople get judged and paid on sales results. So a company culture that is focused on results is healthy and necessary.

The dilemma for sales managers, however, is that a constant push to reach a sales number can keep them and their teams so focused on end goals that they miss opportunities to identify problems with skills and processes so they can improve future results.

Consider this analogy: Imagine that you are a factory manager instead of a sales manager. If your plant isn't meeting its production quota, what would you do? Would you go to the shipping dock and criticize what was being loaded on the trucks? Not likely. You would visit the production lines in the factory and try to pinpoint where the production process was falling apart. Where are the bottlenecks? Where are the mistakes being made?

Too many sales managers I meet don't think like factory managers. They inspect only the final outcome of their sales production line (performance management) rather than what's going on throughout the process. Where were they when the salesperson was making the mistakes that created the poor numbers or the need for a rescue?

When you focus on the inputs to the process, your role as a manager becomes helping your salespeople master **all** of the steps of selling, not just the close. What kinds of inputs are important to sales process results?

- How well sales reps identify customer needs and prioritize the customer's solution criteria

- How well sales reps understand and can explain your solution's competitive advantages

- Whether sales reps can shape a proposal or presentation that presents the best possible case to the customer

To determine if a too-narrow focus on results is an issue for you, ask yourself, "How often am I surprised by a rep's poor performance?" If the answer is "often," then you're looking too much at outcomes and too little at the inputs that produce the outcomes.

Developing Your Leadership Mindsets

How many of these instinct wars did you identify with? I've met very few sales managers who had problems with *all* of the sales instincts I've just covered, but I have also met almost no one who has **none** of these issues. As the classic cartoon character Pogo once said, "We have met the enemy and he is us." So the secret is finding out which one or two sales instincts pose the biggest problem for you and developing a better leadership mindset.

I tell people to think about these instincts like a set of dominoes. Acting on one sales instinct can trigger improvement in all of the other instincts as well. If you can stop that first domino from falling by resisting the temptation to act on a sales instinct, you can prevent a chain reaction of sales behaviors that destroy your leadership opportunity.

To help you get started, I've provided a graphic in Table A where you can rate yourself on each of the instincts covered in this chapter. Simply mark on the lines where you fall between the sales instinct and the leadership mindset.

Table A: Rating Your Instincts

Where do you fall on the spectrum?		
Sales Instinct		**Leadership Mindset**
Be a player		Be an observer
Close deals		Early-cycle sales coaching
Getting tasks done		Developing my people
Pay attention only to results		Also pay attention to inputs

After you've rated yourself, pick the mark that falls closest to the left. Chances are that's the sales instinct you are strongest in. Your challenge on the job and as you read through the rest of this book will be developing concrete steps you can take to shift your mentality to the right, toward the better leadership mindset.

What Contributions Do You Value in Yourself?

Here is one of my favorite quotes about leadership:

"Leadership is a lot like investing in the stock market. If your hope is to make a fortune in a day, you're not going to be successful. There are no successful day traders in leadership."

—**John C. Maxwell,** *The 21 Irrefutable Laws of Leadership*[5]

How about you? Are you a day trader type of sales manager trying to make a big killing in one day? Or are you a long-term investor who is willing to build sustained results? A long-term investor values different things than a day trader, something I hinted at in the discussion of the "closing deals vs. sales coaching" instinct war when I said that Jackie's value used to be in making sales but now had to be in helping others continually improve their sales skills. **The type of contributions you value in yourself as a manager cannot be what you valued in yourself as a salesperson.**

To become a better sales manager, you have to recognize that the best way for you to contribute to your company is not by selling but by developing your ability to assess your sales reps' performances, to pass along your skills through coaching, and to generate continuous improvement in your team.

---

5   John C. Maxwell, *The 21 Irrefutable Laws of Leadership: Follow Them and People Will Follow You* (Thomas Nelson, 2007).

The message I want to drive home is that acting on your finely honed *sales* instincts may feel right in the moment, but it's bad in the long run for your team. There is an old Chinese proverb that is often translated as "a man who chases two rabbits catches neither." You will only continue to put yourself under great stress if you keep trying to sell as well as manage. And the more you continue to sell, the more you'll undermine the confidence of your team. Your salespeople won't get the coaching and support they need. And ultimately you'll see morale go down, turnover go up, and results fall off.

To be a great sales manager, you need to make a commitment to becoming as good (or better) at leadership as you are at selling. Without that commitment, the lessons in this book will be worthless because it's all about *how* you can be a more effective manager and leader. When you come to work every day, focus on what you need to be doing so that your *team* can continually improve—not on how you can win a sale. That's the mindset and commitment of a great sales manager.

Chapter 2
Take Control of Your Time and Priorities

For the past 20-plus years, I've made it a habit to individually inter-view a random selection of sales managers prior to their attendance at my workshops. One question I always ask is, "What is the biggest challenge you face in becoming the best you can be?"

The answer is always the same: *not enough time*.

The simple truth is that all of us have the same amount of time in a day. Yet some sales managers seem to have time for developmental coaching and others don't.

This point really hit home to me when a Fortune 500 company asked me to review its sales manager job description. I saw that about 85 percent of the responsibilities were related to sales coaching.

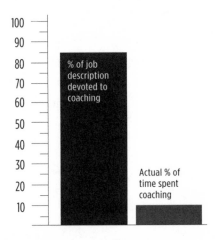

During in-person interviews with this company's regional sales managers, I asked, "What percentage of your time do you spend doing one-on-one coaching with your salespeople?" Not one of the sales managers gave a figure of greater than 10 percent.

In other words, at best 10 percent of a sales manager's day was spent on the tasks associated with achieving 85 percent of what the company expected them to accomplish! These managers spent 90 percent of their time involved in activities unrelated to their highest priorities.

This pattern didn't surprise me. How many times have *you* come into the office with a great plan for the day . . . and by 8:15 a.m. everything blows up in your face? For the rest of the day you chase other people's problems. Suddenly, it's 5:00 p.m. A lot of to-dos were crossed off of other people's lists, but your to-do list was untouched.

The loss of time is a shame. Most sales managers have a lot of knowledge to pass on to their teams, and many have natural coaching skills and feel great pride in teaching others. But somehow they don't have time to use those coaching skills and their teams suffer.

Peter Drucker, the well-known management consultant, once said, "You can't manage time, you can only manage yourself." I agree with him; the topic of time management is really an issue of how you allocate your priorities. Being able to manage time (and thus your priorities) effectively is a prerequisite for being a great sales team leader.

I think of time management as an essential skill for effective sales managers. There's nothing revolutionary about the topic, and no magic tips I can offer that aren't already out there in the marketplace. So, in this chapter, I'm combining my own insights with advice given by the thousands of sales managers I've worked with over the years. I hope this content will help you manage yourself more effectively so you'll have more than 10 percent of your time to devote to improving your salespeople.

Skill 1: Escaping the Reactive Trap

Consider this scenario: One of your salespeople walks into your office saying, "Boss, we have a problem." (Notice their use of the pronoun "we.")

The sales rep blurts out their problem. You say, "Sales rep, let me look into it and I'll get back to you." And in the blink of an eye two things have just happened that are typically associated more with a subordinate than a manager: (1) you accepted a delegation, and (2) you agreed to provide your sales rep with a progress report.

Here's another scenario: You open your email in the morning and find five requests from people who want something from you—information, input on a decision, time for a meeting, something. You naturally respond to all these requests.

This tendency to do first what others ask of you is what I call being caught in a **reactive trap**. You don't have time to do proactive sales coaching because you're too busy solving other people's problems or helping them complete items on *their* to-do list.

Just as with the leadership mindsets I discussed in Chapter 1, salespeople can develop a number of habits that make them prone to getting caught in a reactive mode once they move into management:

1. **"I'm a problem solver!"** Great sales reps didn't get that way by letting problems or challenges slow them down. They jump on the slightest hint of a problem so that something catastrophic doesn't happen. As a sales manager, this mindset becomes "I am 100 percent responsible for solving all team problems." The managers at the aforementioned Fortune 500 company felt that way. And their salespeople did what we'd all do in the same situation: hand off our problems to the manager! Problems in customer service, order entry, you name it. They all got dumped in the sales manager's lap.

   If you solve everyone else's problems guess what your reward is? Yep! Even more "other people's problems" will be dumped on you. (In extreme cases a reactive sales manager becomes like an admin assistant to the sales team—sending a clear message to the team: "Give me all your problems and I will solve them for you." It's like an organizational chart turned upside down.)

2. **"If I solve their problems, my reps can focus on making more sales calls."** If you believe this old wives' tale, I have some bountiful real estate in eastern Nevada to show you. Do you ever wonder what your salespeople are doing after they give you their problems? I don't know for sure what they *are* doing, but decades of experience have taught me they *aren't* making more sales calls!

3. **"I take pride in being decisive."** You were promoted because you are an action-oriented, take-charge person with a high activity level. You've honed the skill of quickly sizing up a situation, making a decision, and moving on. Once again, this sounds like a good characteristic for sales managers, but it suffers from the same issue as item #1 in this list: If *you* make all of the decisions, your team members will never learn how to do it on their own.

4. **"Stress can be intoxicating!"** Many sales managers secretly admit to me that they are adrenaline junkies. They thrived under pressure as a sales rep and want to maintain that sense of excitement as managers. OK, you want your salespeople to have a sense of urgency just like you do. That's fine. I agree that all great salespeople possess a sense of urgency to surpass their sales quotas. But you're not a salesperson anymore! Urgency doesn't help you do a better job or make better decisions, and it certainly doesn't give you more time to develop sales reps' skills and build team morale.

There is a natural human desire to be needed by others, so a sales manager's tendency to get involved in solving problems and making decisions is understandable. But the more you do this, the more you rob yourself of your leadership productivity. When you let any of these mindsets lure you into a reactive trap, you "took the monkey" in the words of Ken Blanchard, the primary author of one of the most successful business books of all time, *The One Minute Manager*. After that book came out, Blanchard did what famous authors do—he came out with a sequel, *The One Minute Manager Meets the Monkey*.[6] In this follow-up book, Blanchard and his coauthors tell us that when one of your people approaches you with a problem, you need to imagine that they have a monkey on their shoulders and that their objective is to get you to take that monkey onto *your* shoulders. Successful managers, says Blanchard et al., don't take that monkey. (See sidebar below.)

I have a more straightforward description: **Don't take on a problem (or task) that is not yours.** Instead, hold your salespeople responsible for solving their own problems.

Passing the monkey

One manager I worked with was so enamored of Ken Blanchard's principle that he borrowed a stuffed monkey from his daughter, discussed the idea with his team, and then put the stuffed monkey on his desk. Thereafter, whenever a rep brought a problem to him, they'd have to acknowledge that "this may be one of those monkeys you talked about!"

---

6   Ken Blanchard, William Oncken Jr., and Hal Burrows, *The One Minute Manager Meets the Monkey* (Quill, 1991).

Sometimes, avoiding the monkey is as simple as not being available every second of every day! A former colleague, Penny, was once the director of sales training for a Fortune 100 company. Before leaving for an exotic vacation, she left a voice mail greeting that said, "I'll be overseas for two weeks and unable to respond to either voice mail or email. If this is important, please speak to my assistant." When she returned from vacation she discovered 93 voice mails! One series of messages was from Joe, one of her regional sales directors. It began two days after Penny left on vacation:

> Day 1: "Penny, this is Joe. We've got an URGENT crisis here. I need to speak to you right NOW! Here's my phone number, cell number, home phone number, wife's cell number. Call me right NOW!"
>
> Day 1 (later): Joe leaves Penny another "urgent" message.
>
> Day 2: Joe calls a third time. "Penny, we're making some progress here, but I'd still like to talk to you."
>
> Day 3: The fourth message from Joe: "Ahhh, Penny, I think we've got it under control. Call me when you get back. Have a nice vacation."

Have you had experiences similar to this? The point is that many problems can be resolved without your involvement. Another point is that if Penny had gotten involved in Joe's crisis, she would have invested a lot of time and energy, and Joe would *not* have learned how to deal with this situation on his own. Plus, spending time on Joe's problems would have prevented Penny from working on her own priorities.

Your skill and, more important, your *will* to resist the instincts that can suck you into a reactive trap are the critical success factors in your ability to devote the time it takes to develop your salespeople into peak sales performers. Choose to step out of this reactive sales management trap.

How? The solution is straightforward: The next time a sales rep approaches you with a problem, don't take the monkey! Don't offer your own opinion right off the bat or allow yourself to be dragged into the drama. The goal should be to help that person figure out a way to deal with the problem on their own. I do this by asking the sales rep what I call the **two magic questions**:

1. What have you done about it so far?

2. What do you think ought to be done next?

I then ask other questions to help shape how the sales rep is approaching the problem but don't offer my own solution.

Using this approach will gradually train your people to understand that if they bring you a fire, they must also bring a possible solution. Pretty soon they'll get the idea that they can resolve many issues themselves without your input.

You can also adopt the role of **fire-preventer-in-chief**. Becoming an excellent firefighter is a mentality that can serve a salesperson well. (See sidebar, p. 36.) As a manager, however, you should *prevent* fires from happening in the first place. So the next time a fire occurs, don't immediately pull out the fire hose. Instead, ask yourself four questions:

1. **What caused this fire?** If you don't think through what caused this problem, you can't prevent it from happening again. Was it a problem with process? Poor communication? Flawed technology?

2. **What were the warning signs?** Looking back, have you seen this problem or others like it occur before? Now that you know what happened, what were the warning signals that something was going wrong?

3. **Is there a way this problem could have been prevented?** Why did this problem come around? What could you have done—or what could you have taught your sales rep—to make sure it didn't happen?

4. **What can you do now to prevent it from recurring?** Typically, you may need to respond by improving the processes your reps use, providing them with training, or providing more consistent coaching.

Perks of a proactive mindset

The more you are able to resist the reactive trap, the more time you'll have to think proactively. This brings many important benefits:

- You won't spend your days doing someone else's job.

- You will lessen the need for reactive firefighting—which means less stress overall, fewer distractions, and more time.

- You'll be able to focus more on *your* priorities and *your* plans.

- Your sales team will feel more empowered to solve their own problems.

Skill 2: Focusing on Priority #1

The Charles Schwab who was the head of Bethlehem Steel in 1932 (*not* the one involved in investing) once challenged a consultant this way: *Show me a way to get more things done with my time. I'll pay you any fee within reason.*

The consultant's advice was that Schwab write down his most important tasks, number them, and then work on Priority #1 until it was done.

Schwab agreed to give it a try. He focused on implementing this simple suggestion and two months later sent the consultant a check for $25,000. (That's $25,000 in 1932 money, which equates today to over $350,000!) So if Charles Schwab thought so highly of this tip to pay $350k for it, that's a pretty good endorsement for us to try this same solution. Agreed?

What is Priority #1 for a sales manager? It has to be **developing salespeople**. You are the only person in the company who can fill that role for your team. And it's the priority that will contribute most to the team's current and future performance and results. This harkens back to the discussion in Chapter 1 about the differences between what salespeople and sales managers should value in themselves. I'll say it again: **Developing your team should be the work you value most in yourself.**

How do you do that? One suggestion is to simply plant your feet and take a stand. Decide here and now that you will coach somebody before noon every day. As the comedian Larry the Cable Guy would say, "Let's get 'er done!"

In the long term, however, the secret lies in separating the *urgent* from the *important*. That's a concept that has been around for decades, usually attributed to a quote by former President Dwight Eisenhower and more recently popularized and operationalized by Stephen Covey in his famous book *The 7 Habits of Highly Effective People.*[7]

---

7   Stephen R. Covey, *The 7 Habits of Highly Effective People: Powerful Lessons in Personal Change* (Simon & Schuster, 2013 [anniversary edition]).

However, I still see plenty of sales managers who are struggling with how to implement that idea. I suggest that they start by reviewing the following list of common tasks that fill sales managers' calendars and then ask themselves, "How many of these activities do I tackle *every day*?"

1. Respond to emails and phone calls.

2. Check sales numbers.

3. Check in with the newest reps or the ones who are struggling the most.

4. Check the status of deals.

5. Respond to boss's requests.

6. Reach out to customers.

7. Spend time doing one-on-one coaching.

8. Link your actions to your company's strategic priorities.

Most managers who give me honest answers confess that they do a lot of the first six activities and not much of the last two (coaching and prioritizing). Why? Because the first six activities always seem urgent (Figure 1); they represent someone standing in front of you (physically or virtually) asking that you do something that *they* want done right away. So the tasks are urgent to someone, just not necessarily important to you!

Figure 1: The Urgent

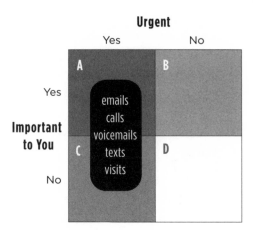

Let me ask you this: **Would any of the first six activities, if you did them effectively and consistently, significantly improve your team's results?** The answer is no. All of those things may feel important or at least urgent in the moment, but none of them have a lasting impact on how well your team performs.

In contrast, the last two items on the list fall into the category of **important but not urgent** (Figure 2). They don't have looming deadlines; there is no one standing in front of you demanding you do coaching right now—but those activities are critical if you want to achieve Priority #1, namely the development of your sales team.

Figure 2: The Important

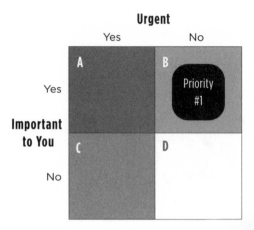

This is why a key strategy in time management is learning to reduce the "urgent/not important to you" tasks (quadrant C) to make room for the "important to you/not urgent" (quadrant B) (Figure 3).

Figure 3: The Challenge

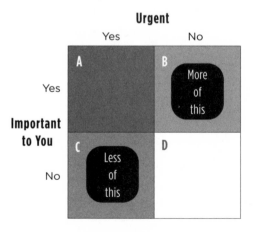

As I discussed earlier in the chapter, one way to tell the difference between an urgent task that is merely a timewaster and a truly important task is who initiates the activity. Timewasters are almost always initiated by someone else, and in responding to them, you are automatically in a reactive mode. Learn to fight the impulse to automatically respond to every request that comes your way . . . the desire to answer every email, every text, every call . . . the instinct to fight every fire that you're called in to fight.

To meet this challenge, start by examining a typical day or week and think about how you actually spend your time. Create a blank matrix and write down your daily tasks in the appropriate quadrant (or use the Eisenhower app![8]). Identify the biggest timewasters (the "urgent/not important to you" tasks). If you can manage those factors, you'll have a lot more time for coaching and leading. (See sidebar below.)

Treat coaching like an airplane flight

Every month, I have 8 to 10 appointments that I am never, ever late for, regardless of what is going on or what is "incoming." These include airplane flights—because the consequences of not getting to where I need to go are immediate and dramatic. If you can convince yourself that coaching your team is as important a priority as making an airplane flight, you'll be in good shape.

---

8   http://www.eisenhower.me/

Skill 3: Become a Master of Time Management

Today's sales managers face an ever-increasing array of interruptions in their day: emails, tweets, calls, texts, drop-in visitors. While some people seem to thrive amidst that chaos, studies summarized in *Harvard Business Review* in 2013[9] indicate that people who "chronically multi-tasked failed to allocate resources in a way that matches their priorities." Further, the constant interruptions are not good for clear thinking. "The fractured nature of modern work is a tremendous burden. . . . The resulting mental fatigue takes its toll in forms of mistakes, shallow thinking, and impaired self-regulation. . . . We go on autopilot and our brains fall back to simply responding to whatever is in front of us, regardless of its importance."

The solution? Take steps to make sure your day is not quite so fractured, which means managing your time more effectively. To do that you'll need to address any underlying challenges that cause you to waste time, such as these:

- Being unorganized (searching for files, not controlling your calendar, etc.)

- Not having well-defined processes (having to reinvent the wheel with each new problem)

Addressing these issues fully is beyond the scope of this book, but here are some tried-and-true strategies to get you started:

1. **Collect** things that need to be done. Clearly define what needs doing. If the action item requires less than two minutes of effort, just do it. If it is trash, trash it.

---

9   Adam Waytz and Malia Mason, "Your Brain at Work," *Harvard Business Review*, July/August 2013.

2. **Organize** things. Sort items by response time or category, delegate what you can, and store non-actionable items (as data in your CRM tool).

3. **Review** things. Continue to update with new info, ideas, changes, etc.

4. **Create action plans.** Make decisions about implementation, tools to use, and resources required. (See sidebar below.)

If time management is a challenge for you, here are the tricks and tips that have proven most helpful to the sales managers I've worked with.

Goals, priorities, and action

Chapter 10 is devoted to the topic of identifying break-through goals for your team and creating action plans to achieve those goals. Having a written plan can serve as a constant reminder to you about your most important priorities, which should help you make better decisions day in and day out (and even in times of stress) about the best use of your time.

Tip 1: Tame the email/text/voice mail monsters

A sales manager recently told me that she sends and receives, on average, 100 emails every day, which takes about two hours of her time. That equates to 500 hours per year that she spends on email, or 62½ work days. Imagine if she could reduce the amount of time spent on email by 33 percent. That one change alone could give her an additional 20 days per year of additional time for coaching salespeople!

No discussion of time management for sales managers would be complete without addressing the issue of email overload. Without a doubt, the huge amount of time spent handling volumes of emails and texts is the number one challenge that sales managers tell me they face in terms of their efforts to get smarter about time. But consider this: Few sales teams that I know of have ever moved from good to great because their sales manager answered a lot of emails quickly.

My top tip is to **stop doing email/voice mail first thing in the morning**. You know what happens when you check your email. There's some hair-on-fire issue waiting in your in-box that demands your immediate attention. But 9 times out of 10, it's a distraction that is important to somebody else but not to you. And once you head off down that road, another distraction pops up that prevents you from getting back to your priorities.

Here are some additional email tips:

- Set team expectations around the use of email/texts.

  › Keep them short and to the point.

  › Be specific about what you need.

  › Be specific about timeline.

  › Write clear, descriptive email titles/subjects for sorting capability.

  › Use NRN (no reply needed) when appropriate.

- Decide what your high-priority activities are **before** you check your email/voice mails/texts each day.

- Write clear, concise, actionable emails. Tell the person what they need to know and what you need from them.

- Do not send thank-yous for everything.

- Color-code your incoming email (e.g., make emails from your boss red).

- Set team standards regarding copying others on emails and consider the "reply all" button as a potential timewaster. Coach others to send you more actionable, less informational email.

- Use the status options for texting (Do Not Disturb).

And finally, **send** fewer emails yourself! You set the tone for your team. If you send a lot of emails, and they're long and drawn out, well, you'll receive more long and drawn out messages.

Dealing with too many calls is much the same. Here are some solutions managers have shared with me to deal with the issue:

- Let calls go to voice mail.

- Set a specific time each day when you will listen to and answer voice mail messages.

- Use the Do Not Disturb phone feature when possible.

- Give your number only to key people.

- Condition sales reps/other employees to expect reasonable but not instantaneous response times.

Tip 2: Prioritize your to-do list

The *Harvard Business Review* article I referenced earlier in this chapter had another conclusion that is critical for sales managers: "Success as a leader requires, first and foremost, creating just a few clear priorities and gathering the courage to eliminate or outsource less-important tasks and goals."

To make this advice actionable, I suggest you start to **prioritize your to-do lists**: Write down a list of daily tasks and prioritize them from most to least important. Then work on the number one task until it's done (remember Charles Schwab's advisor!).

The trick is to review the list and ask yourself:

- Which of these activities is most important?

- What can be safely postponed?

- What can I delegate?

- Is there a way I can respond to this timewaster in such a way that developmental coaching of a salesperson occurs?

By asking yourself these questions, you are well on your way to having more time to devote to becoming a more proactive manager and strategic sales coach.

Great managers take this practice a step further by developing their own **to-don't** list, as well. At the end of the workday, they reflect back and ask themselves, "What did I do today that did *not* have a meaningful impact on the growth of my team?" Perhaps they got distracted by a customer problem that could have been handled by a salesperson or allowed themselves to be interrupted by someone who was not on their sales team. They learn to identify these timewasters and stop allowing themselves to become distracted. Fewer timewasters means more time for coaching.

When an urgent-to-someone-else issue presents itself, just say no (unless it truly is a crisis). Better yet, shut off your cell phone, get out of your office, and get yourself into a coaching situation with one of your sales reps.

By appointment only

Another trick of time management that many sales managers use to avoid distractions is to set appointments on their calendar for specific tasks, not just events.

- Have designated hours, reserved on your calendar, that are "open door" (anyone can come to talk about anything, including problems). Teach your team to use those times to discuss urgent issues rather than sending emails/texts or calling.

- Reserve coaching times well ahead of time, and perhaps as a regular appointment (I'd like to see you reserve an hour each morning for coaching). Again, you train your team to know that you're not available during those hours.

Tip 3: Be more deliberate about meeting time

Another bugaboo in office environments—not just sales—are ubiquitous meetings that accomplish little. Having your team together in the same room (physically or virtually) is a precious resource that should be treated accordingly and not squandered. Try these tips to make your meetings more effective:

- Make sure that a meeting is needed. Is there some advantage to having people all together discussing an idea or hearing information *at the same time?* If not, perhaps other forms of communication would work.

- At least several days in advance of the meeting, send out an agenda with the following elements:

  › Identifies all topics to be discussed and action goals (define next steps, make a decision, etc.). Flag one topic as the top priority.

  › Includes links to any background reading (reports, histories, recommendations) to be reviewed in advance.

  › Requests people to bring other pertinent information to the meeting.

- Start all meetings on time even if some people are missing. Your sales reps will soon get the message to respect everyone else's time.

- Reduce your typical meeting time, say from one hour to 45 minutes, to allow less time for tangents.

- Review the objectives at the start of the meeting and ask for comments/additions.

- Assign a note taker to capture decisions made, next steps, responsibilities.

- Manage the agenda. If an item is taking longer than planned, make the call on whether to shorten the discussion on other items, or to wrap it up and continue the topic at the next meeting.

- Get feedback after the meeting. What went well? What could have been improved? Implement those lessons for the next meeting.

Now, About Your Leadership Destiny . . .

As I hope I've made clear in this chapter, you simply cannot achieve your full potential as a sales team leader if you spend the bulk of your time in reactive mode—solving everyone else's problems, holding ineffective meetings, shuffling through papers, or dealing with any other number of timewasters. You need to make sure you have plenty of time to plan, coach, measure, and manage. *These are the priorities for sales management leadership.*

It is these choices you make every day—to be reactive or proactive, to accept or reject the monkeys that people try to pass off to you, to adhere to a to-don't list as well as a to-do list—wherein lies your leadership destiny.

Section 2

Elements of Excellence

Overview

This section is all about excellence: developing excellence, hiring excellence, and selling excellence.

The thing about excellence is that it's not a matter of random chance. Any team can have one great quarter. An excellent team is one that can have one great quarter after another. So the underlying themes here are around processes and replication: I don't want you to develop one great sales rep; I want you to be able to develop all of your sales reps into peak performers. I don't want you to hire one promising candidate; I want you to increase the odds that every hire will be a great fit for your team. I don't want the occurrence of a big sale to feel so random; I want all of your sales reps to be more effective in dealing with customers in every opportunity going forward.

The three chapters in this section will help you create a solid foundation for excellence:

Chapter 3: Drive Rep Accountability for Breakthrough Sales Performance discusses the impossibility of holding reps fully accountable for their performance unless there is a clear description of what exactly excellence should look like. High expectations that are well communicated to your team are an essential component of a high-performance culture.

Chapter 4: Hire Smarter addresses a fundamental dilemma all sales managers face, namely that the best coaching in the world is not going to rescue someone who is ill-suited for the job. This chapter discusses how to evaluate candidates to make sure you are bringing on "A-players" (people who are a good fit for the job and the team).

Chapter 5: Insert the Customer in Your Sales Process points out that many companies deploy a sales model that is missing a critical element—the customer. Without a deep understanding of customer buying, your sales reps will find that success and failure are often inexplicable: Why did one deal go through and another fall off the cliff? Having a sales process structured around your customer's buying process will strengthen all aspects of how your reps approach sales opportunities and how you manage the team (including making your customer relationship management, or CRM, system more relevant to salespeople so they are more likely to use it, and improving forecast accuracy).

Chapter 3

Drive Rep Accountability for Breakthrough Sales Performance

Ask a sales rep about accountability and there may not be any outright swearing, but the words they use will not be flattering.

I can understand that reaction. Accountability is a word that sales managers often toss around when they want to place blame for something that has gone wrong. "I'm going to hold you accountable for those poor results!"

When done right, accountability can be key to developing a highly professional and productive sales team. When done wrong, it can ruin morale and undermine sales results.

Unfortunately, accountability is in a sorry state in most companies. The core problem is illustrated by the work of Columbia University researcher Ferd Fournies who surveyed about 25,000 managers[10] over a number of years. He asked them why they thought employees often didn't meet expectations for their jobs and to provide specific examples

---

10 Ferdinand Fournies, *Coaching for Improved Work Performance* (McGraw-Hill, 2000), 93–95.

of where employees fell short. Here are the top three answers in no particular order. Can you guess which one ranked first?

a. Don't know HOW to do their jobs

b. Don't know WHAT to do

c. Don't know WHY they should do a particular task

The answer is (b)—employees don't know what to do. In fact, not only did that answer rate highest overall but it also was no lower than second on 99 percent of the surveys. What is interesting, as Fournies points out, is that "when managers try to solve individual performance problems, they *rarely* select [don't know what they are supposed to do] as the place to start to solve the problem." That is, the first step in trying to resolve a performance issue is never making sure that the employee knows what to do.

Though this study wasn't done specifically in sales, I think the results are a powerful eye-opener for all managers. How can we possibly hold sales reps accountable if we haven't taught them *what* they are supposed to do—that is, what they are accountable for?

And by *what*, I don't mean just their specific tasks or responsibilities; I mean what level of performance is expected in order to succeed on the team. A sales rep, for example, knows that one *what* is "generate leads." But how many leads over what time frame would indicate that they are thriving on the job? What level would indicate that they are struggling?

I know you're probably thinking that you have clearly defined *what* your salespeople need to do in the form of job descriptions. I recognize that most companies have job descriptions, but often those are either outdated or not specific enough for the purpose of managing a sales team. Further, even in companies with detailed job descriptions, the sales managers tell me that they only refer to the description when they either hire or fire someone.

Some companies tell me they have defined the *what* of sales rep performance through standards. But when I dig a little deeper, a number of sales managers will admit they really haven't done a good job of identifying the standards they want their salespeople to meet. Others tell me they have standards but haven't communicated them other than establishing a sales quota.

All of this tells me that few companies have done a great job of helping their sales reps understand the *what* part of their job. That is, sales reps don't know exactly what it is they are going to be held accountable for besides their sales numbers. If you do not communicate your expectations and standards—and then blame people for missing them—you'll create a very negative dynamic on your team.

In the rest of this chapter, I'll talk about actions you can take to fill this void:

- Setting high standards

- Clearly defining expectations for the sales rep job

- Effectively communicating those expectations to your team

- Evaluating performance to determine whether reps are meeting those expectations

Once you have these components in place, you can establish a higher degree of accountability around standards of excellence—a surefire recipe for driving breakthrough performance.

Raising the Bar

When I ask sales managers to describe their performance expectations, they almost always show me numbers that are considered the **minimum acceptable levels**. Translation: If you, the salesperson, don't do *at least* this much, you're out of a job.

Setting only minimum standards is like telling someone to run in a race and coaching them only enough so that they don't come in last! What kind of motivation is that? If all of your team members were only meeting the minimum, you wouldn't be very happy, would you? So while you may need to define minimum levels to satisfy your organization's human resources policies, do not use them for setting expectations.

As one sales VP said to me, "Our sales managers won't fire anyone for achieving the minimums, but we don't want any team to think that's all they need to do. I want to raise the bar so all our teams know exactly what it will take to excel at the job." He's right. The idea here is that you want to define performance in a way that will let your people know what greatness looks like! You want **standards of excellence**, not standards of "at least I won't be fired."

Characteristics of a peak performer

What does it mean to have standards of excellence on a sales team? Think of it this way: If I asked you what your top producer does differently and how you can help everybody else on the team to aspire to those standards of excellence set by your top producer, what would you say?

Every sales manager is, has been, or has known someone who was a peak performer. So one way to start answering my question is to think about characteristics you exhibit or that a peak performer you know exhibits. Here are some common answers:

- Good communicator

- Organized

- Negotiates well

- Great selling skills

- Develops killer proposals/presentations

- Good work ethic, self-motivated

- Positive attitude

- Team player

- Competitive

- Honest

- Creative

- Problem solver

There's something interesting about this list that most sales managers don't give serious consideration to until it's pointed out to them. Implicitly, they have equated sales effectiveness not just with specific **skills** (the first five items on the list) but also with a number of **will** or **attitude** characteristics (the next five items)—plus a couple of characteristics that represent a combination of skill and will (the last two items).

I then ask the managers to indicate which of these characteristics they think are *most important* for a sales rep's success, and guess what? Most of them choose the attitudes and wills. In fact, they tell me that about 60 percent to 70 percent of job success is due to having a positive attitude.

Once they've had this revelation, I then ask, "How many of these characteristics are in your job descriptions? Your hiring criteria? Your evaluation forms?" Usually, they pick out three or four skills but few if any wills. So attitude is important but we're not looking for it when hiring? When doing evaluations? When coaching?

This gap is another reason why I believe most companies haven't sufficiently described the *what* part of the sales rep job. Even in companies that have done a decent job of describing critical skills, they are likely missing out on what could well be 60 percent to 70 percent of what it takes to be a peak performer—all of the wills or attitudes.

The main lesson is that to be a sales manager who can develop peak performers, you'll need to focus on both skills and wills in your team. Let's start with the simpler part of that equation.

Defining Skills for Excellence

For the purposes of this book, I'm going to assume you have existing job descriptions that likely spell out many of the skills you're looking for from your sales reps. Use that as a starting point, but be aware you may need to flesh out the list. An example from one company is shown in Figure 4.

Once you develop your own list of skills, I challenge you to take another look at them and see if (a) they capture all of the most critical skills necessary for the job and (b) they are up to date based on your company's current needs.

The key words in item (a) are "all of the most critical skills." Don't try to be too exhaustive in your list but make sure you haven't overlooked anything that reps really need. One example is shown in Figure 4. As you can see, this company decided to define two different kinds of skills: those associated with using their sales process and those that are more general.

The importance of item (b) was made evident to me when I was talking with a sales VP who worked for a company that had undergone some major shifts in recent years. The market was expanding, partly through increased specialization of offerings. I asked him to share with me the job descriptions for his sales reps, and it turned out they had not been updated to reflect the company's shift in focus and changes in the marketplace. "I guess it's unfair to ding sales reps when we as a company haven't clearly defined their jobs," the sales VP said. "We need to have much more specialized job descriptions."

Figure 4

Skills

SALES PROCESS SKILLS

Connects with prospects based on knowledge of their business needs

Uses telephone prospecting scripts

Uses diagnostic questioning to identify multiple needs and the ripple effects

Shapes customer criteria in ways that favor our differentiators

Shapes an effective strategy to beat the competition

Prepares a persuasive presentation/proposal

Helps customers resolve their fears and concerns

Deals with customer negotiating tactics

Creates customer loyalty and grows the account through post-sale support

GENERAL SELLING SKILLS

Knowledge of our products/services

Listens to and connects with customers

Can identify what step of buying a customer is in

Keeps customers moving forward through their buying process

Makes connections with more than one decision maker in an account
(as appropriate)

Overall professionalism

Creativity

Responds to customer requests

To make that happen, the sales VP reviewed the existing job descriptions with each sales manager, who, in turn, discussed the descriptions with sales reps who were successful at selling the new specialized solutions and asked them to point out anything and everything they did that *wasn't* in the description. The managers then reported back to the sales VP, and together they developed new, more relevant and complete job descriptions.

Defining "Wills" for Excellence

As with skills, the goal here is to define the will or attitude characteristics that are needed for success on your team. Again, if you think about the best performers you know, you can probably come up with a list of wills or attitudes. An example list is shown in Figure 5.

Figure 5

Will (positive attitude)

Prospects consistently

Enthusiasm for resolving customer problems/complaints

Strong work ethic (hardworking and diligent)

Strong initiative (can work effectively without being told what to do)

Competitive drive

Results-oriented

A positive influence on coworkers

Learns quickly/coachable

Tenacious (keeps focused until an outcome is achieved)

Constantly looks for opportunities to learn and improve

You can't stop at just developing the list, however. Just as you can't measure a skill like "being organized" unless you know what you're looking for, the same holds true for wills. You need to make sure that the attitudinal qualities you want to see in your sales reps are clearly defined so *you* know how to observe and evaluate them and *your reps* have a fuller picture of the job expectations.

The best way I've found for sales managers to develop a useful definition of a will is to think about the **behaviors** they will see if a rep exhibits that will. Some examples are shown in Table B.

Table B: Observing Wills in Action

Will	Observable behaviors
Competitive	Hates to lose. Constantly working on getting better.
Good work ethic	High activity level. Determined to complete tasks. Hates to miss quota.
Problem solver	Accepts responsibility for solving problems. Can define the problem's causes and solutions. Understands that their solution can't create more problems for coworkers.

Creating and Using a Success Profile

The most effective way I know to translate information on skills or wills (which collectively reflect your standards of excellence) is to create a document called a **Success Profile**. At a minimum, the form should include your lists of skills and wills like those shown in Figure 4 and Figure 5, plus a third element: the performance standards you want to establish for sales results and activity levels. (Remember, you want to have high standards, not settle for the minimum levels). An example template for this third element is shown in Figure 6.

Figure 6: Success Profile for Sales Representatives

For the sales managers: Fill in a form like this that defines measurable/observable outcomes that you expect sales reps to achieve.

Sales Results

1. Meets or exceeds monthly/quarterly/annual quota of _____ (dollars/units/ product mix).
2. Brings in _____ (#) new customers/accounts per _____(quarter/year).
3. Sells value and exceeds company targets for gross profit.

Sales Process Activity

4. Completes _____ (#) prospecting calls per week/month.
5. Delivers _____ (#) proposals/presentations per week/month.
6. Follows up on _____ (%) of leads within _____ (#) hours/days.

Account Development

7. Develops account penetration plans for growing revenue from major accounts.
8. Has a strong relationship with at least one sponsor in each account.
9. Contacts primary account contact at least ____ (#) times per month/quarter.

Team Member Responsibilities

10. Keeps CRM database updated (contacts, decision maker interests/concerns).
11. Reviews processes and results regularly to identify improvements.
12. Controls expenses.
13. Adheres to company policies, guidelines, processes, and ethical codes.
14. Keeps up to date on product/service updates and releases.
15. Attends _____ (#) professional development opportunities per year and/or engages in other industry-specific professional development.

Having a written document like this is critical to being consistent in your communicating and coaching with reps. But once you have a Success Profile, what do you do with it?

Using a Success Profile

One of my former employers had a strict rule: Every manager was to have an annual performance review from their boss no later than February 15. The CEO would then receive a list of names on February 16 of the bosses who had not completed reviews of their managers—and that was not the kind of recognition that the bosses wanted to receive!

So every year around February 12 I would get a message from my boss, the Area VP, instructing me to meet him at the Delta Crown Room at San Diego International Airport. He'd fly in, meet with me for about an hour, complete my review, then jump back on the plane and head off to another airport to meet with another one of his managers, hoping to meet the CEO's deadline.

During the meeting, he would proceed to tell me all the things that he wished I had been doing differently the previous year. And every time, it was like he had been saving up his opinions, waiting for this moment to render judgment. As I'd listen to his evaluation, one question would always keep popping up in my mind: *Why didn't you tell me this earlier when I could have done something about it?* I always felt alienated and angry. It was very demotivating!

With a Success Profile you are in a better position to prevent this kind of demotivating situation from ever happening. Use it as the basis for more frequent—and meaningful—discussions with each of your reps. The profile helps you focus on specific development needs, which means your comments will more likely be viewed as helpful feedback than after-the-fact criticism.

To make this happen, start by adding an assessment component to the form. Figure 7, for example, depicts the will section shown earlier, but with the "performs well" and "needs work" columns added. Other companies prefer to have a numerical rating system (such as 1 = poor to 5 = excellent).

Figure 7: Using a Success Profile for Assessment

Will (positive attitude)

	Performs Well	Needs Work
Prospects consistently		
Enthusiasm for resolving customer problems/ complaints		
Strong work ethic (hard-working and diligent)		
Strong initiative (can work effectively without being told what to do)		
Competitive drive		
Results-oriented		
A positive influence on coworkers		
Learns quickly/coachable		
Tenacious (keeps focused until an outcome is achieved)		
Constantly looks for opportunities to learn and improve		

After you've developed an assessment-focused Success Profile, hand it to a rep and nonchalantly say something like: "In order for me to help you with a personalized developmental plan, I want you to complete this simple tool by rating yourself in these areas. I'll do the same[11] and we'll get together for lunch next week and talk about it, OK?"

It is vital that you have the right mindset for this discussion. It is not a performance review. The purpose is to help the rep improve. After this meeting, you should be able to create an individual development plan focusing on two or three skills or wills for improvement.

During the discussion, ask the rep to share their own ratings first (this will help build their self-evaluation skills). Ask questions or point out issues or differences you noted in your own ratings. Then ask them to identify two or three areas that they think they need to work on most. Determine action steps the rep will commit to and a timeline for implementation.

Six months later, repeat the exercise, but give each rep a copy of their original ratings as well as a blank form. Ask them to review the ratings they gave themselves earlier and then rate themselves again on each skill and will. After you've rated them again, as well, have another conversation—only this time, start by asking, "If *you* were *me*, what would you advise at this point?" Discuss their evaluation of how much progress they've made and what they need to focus on next. Continue this cycle every three to six months. This regular review will help reinforce the well-rounded definition of success that you want for your team.

When you have this kind of system in place, your reps will benefit from knowing exactly what it is they are supposed to achieve (this helps new hires, too, as described in the sidebar, p. 68). A few years ago, for example, one of my clients asked me to help them evaluate the impact of the training I had just delivered to their sales managers. I recommended that they look at the impact on the sales reps of having managers who were better trained on coaching skills. One of the key results is depicted in Figure 8, which shows that nearly 85 percent of the sales reps had a

---

11 I think it works best if the sales manager rates the sales rep, too, but some managers choose to just review the rep's self-ratings.

better understanding of what they needed to improve as a result of more regular conversations with their managers focused on the Success Profile.

Figure 8: Impact on Reps of Using Success Profiles

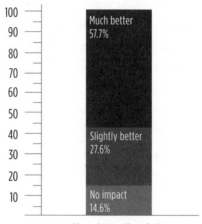

Now that's the kind of manager that I'd like to work for!

Starting off on the right foot

You can also use the Success Profile to help new sales-people understand the full range of expectations for the job they've just taken. Imagine bringing a new hire on and being able to show them your Success Profile. You can say to them, "These are the characteristics and attributes of the best people who have worked here. I want you to join their ranks, so my job is to describe for you what these standards are and help you achieve them."

Now that's the kind of manager that I'd like to work for!

Accountability for the Future

Let me end this chapter by going back to the very beginning. Do you remember the number one answer for why employees don't meet expectations? It was because they don't know *what* to do. If you have a Success Profile and use it regularly to communicate standards, evaluate your salespeople, and identify improvement priorities for each individual, then you have answered the *what* question. When asked, "What is expected of you?" your team will be able to answer with a much more complete answer than simply "make quota."

There's a common theme running throughout this book: Great sales managers look more to the future than the past. As I pointed out at the beginning of this chapter, accountability is commonly perceived as a negative because sales managers apply the concept toward the past—they hold sales reps accountable for numbers, which reflect only past performance.

By using a Success Profile to communicate your expectations to reps, you're telling them ahead of time what they will be held accountable for in the future. That's how accountability becomes a positive force on a sales team, and it completely changes the dynamics between a manager and a rep. When everyone on your team understands what excellence looks like, you will see these benefits:

- You can hold them accountable to higher standards.

- Your reps are more likely to aspire to greatness.

- You can keep them focused on the skills and behaviors they need to pay attention to.

Chapter 4

Hire Smarter

We all know the cost of a bad hiring decision . . . or do we?

Some years ago, I was standing at the bar in the Acapulco Princess Hotel along with a number of fellow employees. We had won our company's "incentive trip" awarded to top employees. I was a sales general manager at the time.

As I stood there chatting, a gentleman who looked vaguely familiar walked up to me. He was smiling as he said, "Do you remember me?"

"You do look familiar," I replied.

He told me that two and a half years ago I had interviewed him for a sales position but decided not to hire him. "Shortly after that," he said, "I moved to Dallas and signed on with the company. And here I am."

It dawned on me that in just about two years, he'd done well enough with our company to rank among the top 5 percent of 1,500 salespeople. And I had rejected him. Ironic, given I was in Mexico because of my success as a sales manager.

I turned to the bartender and ordered another shot of tequila.

Every time I talk with sales managers, I ask them if there is someone on their team, right now, they wish they hadn't hired. Nearly every single manager says yes. They know that hiring the wrong people is very costly in terms of time, opportunity cost, lost salary, and potentially damaged morale. Perhaps that's why most of us equate "bad hiring decisions" with the people we bring on who turn out to be poor performers.

But back at that bar in Mexico so many years ago, I'd come face to face with one of my biggest hiring mistakes, a gem that I had let slip through my fingers.

It is impossible to overstate the importance of getting hiring decisions right. Everything else in your job is going to be tougher and other strategies may ultimately be unsuccessful if you get that very first decision wrong.

The key to avoiding both types of hiring mistakes is consistency and methodology. We all know that our salespeople do better if they use a consistent approach to selling, that if they miss steps, they will have a greater chance of losing the sale. The same principle applies here. You need to have a consistent process to improve your chances of hiring the right people instead of the wrong people. How to improve your hiring process is the topic of this chapter.

Asking the Right Questions

A decade ago, human resources consultant Leigh Branham published *The 7 Hidden Reasons Employees Leave*,[12] which examined factors that drive employees to look for new jobs. The top two reasons from the survey he conducted were as follows:

1. Job or workplace was not what was expected

2. Mismatch between the job and the person

In my mind, it's clear that both of these reasons are linked to poor hiring processes. The company either did not know how to describe the workplace and the job correctly, did not know how to evaluate

---

12   Leigh Branham, *The 7 Hidden Reasons Employees Leave: How to Recognize the Subtle Signs and Act Before It's Too Late* (AMACOM, 2005).

candidates for the required job, or did a poor job of communicating expectations and job requirements to the candidate.

This survey demonstrates that, when it comes to hiring, the job of a sales manager must go beyond asking good questions in a job interview. Managers must be able to define what is required for the job (as I discussed in Chapter 3) and develop ways to assess whether a candidate will be a good fit.

As you may have guessed from reading the previous chapter, in my view the starting point for having a more effective hiring process is a Success Profile that describes both the skills and wills that people need for the job of sales rep in your company. That profile will help you document what specific skills and attitudes you are looking for in job candidates. But for hiring purposes, you need to add two more categories:

1. Evaluating whether the person is a good fit, culturally, for your team and your company

2. Evaluating a candidate's wills and especially their coachability (openness to learning and improving)

Let's look at how these additional categories can improve your hiring decisions.

Evaluating Cultural Fit

"Cultural fit" sounds like a squishy subject, doesn't it? It can be, unless you take the extra steps to define what it means to you. Just as you did with the wills part of the Success Profile, you need to identify specific behaviors and attitudes that represent what you want to see, or you won't be able to evaluate whether or not a candidate possesses them.

Start by thinking about the adjectives you'd use to describe the culture of your company and team. Then think about ways that you could tell whether a candidate would function well in that environment. Table C shows some common examples.

Table C: Examples of Evaluating Cultural Fit

Adjective/ descriptor for your company	How to evaluate fit
Team player	Ask the person to compare the difference between a rep's responsibility to themselves vs. to their team. Do they have examples of collaboration with coworkers?
Entrepreneurial spirit	Listen for the passion (or lack of it) in their voice as they talk about sales as a profession. Ask the person to describe their career path (you'd be looking for someone who has clear goals and ambitions). Ask for examples of jobs or tasks they've undertaken that were outside their job duties—are there any signs that they are a self-starter?
Goal-oriented	Ask the person to give examples of the goals they set for themselves in their current or previous position. How do they use those goals (e.g., to focus their efforts, set priorities)? Did they achieve the goals?
Continually improving	Ask the person to give examples of how they've improved in the last year. How did they identify what to work on? How did they evaluate their progress? What happened after they made one improvement—did they look for the next thing?
Accountable	When the person is describing experiences at their current or previous position, listen for language that indicates they took responsibility for the results, good or bad. Do they acknowledge their own mistakes or blame poor performance on their job circumstances?

Another approach is to dig for specifics of what the candidate likes and doesn't like in a work environment. For example, I read in *USA Today* that the number one reason productive people leave an organization is because of their relationship with their immediate supervisor. So ask the candidate this question:

Describe a sales manager whose style conflicted with yours.

This question probes their relationship with previous managers and can help you understand what is important to them in a work environment. You'll hear about what types of things a sales manager has done that wasn't helpful to them, and you can compare that to how you like to manage.

(I like this question for another reason: It gets the candidate to talk about someone other than themselves. Too often when interviewing we fall into the trap of asking questions that require answers dealing only with the candidate's experience or thoughts. To answer this question, they have to talk about how they interacted with others in the workplace.)

The Importance of Wills and Coachability

Obviously, I can't know what attitudes you'll want in your sales reps, but in this section I'll cover a variety of examples and provide tips on what you can do in an interview to determine if the person possesses those characteristics.

1. Enthusiasm and dedication

With Internet searches being so easy these days, it's safe to assume that your candidates will have at least done a quick search on your company. What you want to know is how *much* research a candidate has done. So try asking something like this:

> *What research have you done on our company? What did you find out?*

This question takes candidates beyond their prepared answers about your company by asking them to describe not only what information was gathered but also the process they went through to compile it. Underperformers visited your company's home web page and simply mined a few factoids to sprinkle in your meeting. The candidate you want went far beyond that in their preparation.

2. Drive to achieve results

Most interviewers will include a general question about what a candidate has achieved in prior positions. What I'd like you to do is push for details by asking this question:

> *Give me an example of some specific results you achieved in your most recent sales position.*

Successful salespeople will be able to give you plenty of those specific details. Less successful salespeople may offer some initial specifics, no doubt well rehearsed, but then tend to shift the discussion away from the question or will talk about team goals achieved (not emphasizing their individual contribution). These less-desirable candidates will also be somewhat vague.

3. Analytical ability

To be successful, a sales rep needs to be able to analyze a customer's situation, including identifying all of the complex factors that may be at work (varying requirements, different decision makers, etc.). One way to evaluate a candidate's analytical capabilities during the interview is to find out how much they have thought through their current job search. For example, you could ask this:

> *What criteria are important to you in selecting your next sales opportunity?*

The depth of thinking in their answer reveals how much thought they have put into their next career move. That can give you a good indication of how deeply they think through situations and how good a match your opening is to what they are looking for.

4. Evaluating coachability

While it's true that some sales reps are naturals and likely will succeed in almost all situations, those self-driven top performers are more the exception than the rule. Most reps require sales coaching to attain top skills and performance levels.

What is coachability? When I ask sales managers this question, most of the time there is confusion regarding the correct definition. A large percentage say they are looking for someone who has an agreeable personality and listens attentively, but in my experience, an agreeable person is not necessarily coachable.

Coachability is tied to personality traits such as willingness to change, openness to feedback and ideas from others, positive acceptance of constructive criticism, interest in continued improvement, and motivation to succeed and constantly strive for new challenges and results. People with these traits will not just listen to advice but commit to *applying* it. (See sidebar, p. 79.) If a sales rep doesn't have these kinds of traits, your coaching will have little impact.

Mark Roberge, currently the chief revenue officer for HubSpot's Sales Division and author of *The Sales Acceleration Formula*, found that coachability was the trait most closely correlated with sales success. So it became the single most significant factor in his hiring decisions. In his book, Roberge describes how he would use role-playing during interviews not so much to test the candidate's skill but to see how well they could take advice.[13] He would set up a scenario that was something the candidate could encounter if brought onboard—such as talking to an executive who had already downloaded an article from HubSpot's website. Roberge would ask the candidate to role-play doing some "light discovery" with the goal of getting this executive to agree to an appointment.

Following the role-play, Roberge would ask, "How do you think you did?" (This tests the candidate's ability to self-evaluate.) He would listen to the response to see how well the candidate could evaluate their own performance. Roberge writes: "If the person said, 'I think I did great,' that was a *bad* sign." He wanted to hear details from the candidate about what they did right and what they could have improved.

Roberge wasn't done yet, though. He would outline a strength and suggest a few improvements for the candidate. **He would then ask the candidate to redo the role-play**, this time attempting to apply some of the coaching he had just provided.

The key message here is that you shouldn't waste time and resources hiring salespeople who can't or won't grow on the job and end up taking up valuable space on your sales team. That's why evaluating coachability when hiring is so important.

---

13   Mark Roberge, *The Sales Acceleration Formula: Using Data, Technology, and Inbound Selling to Go from $0 to $100 Million* (Wiley, 2015), 13–15.

Hungry and humble

Like many people, I'm a big fan of March Madness and followed the exploits of the Villanova Wildcats in the 2016 NCAA basketball tournament. Along with the rest of America, I was thrilled by the last-second three-point shot that won them the championship. Their achievement impressed me so much that I decided to study up on the team coach, Jay Wright.

Wright has said that when doing recruiting, he looks for players who are both hungry and humble, and he uses variations on the motto "stay humble, stay hungry" as part of this coaching strategy.

I think the hungry part we all get. We all want players on our team who are driven to win and motivated to achieve great things.

But what about humble? That struck me as odd. I'd have thought he'd want players who were perhaps bold and brash, whose self-confidence could carry them through tough times. But Wright has great insight. He says that if a player does not have humility, they won't be coachable. And what good is a player who isn't coachable?

Sales managers are increasingly telling me that they're starting to pay more attention to coachability when they look for new hires—mostly because they're tired of dealing with sales reps who refuse to listen to advice. I think that's a wise move. Maybe we all need more humble players on our teams.

The Hiring Process

A Success Profile that describes what is needed to thrive on your team, plus a solid idea of what skills and wills you want to evaluate (and how to evaluate them), arms you with knowledge that will help you shape a better hiring process. Now, let's focus on three critical aspects of the hiring process itself: (1) how you screen out bad candidates and screen in the good, (2) how to make the actual interviews more revealing, and (3) what you can do beyond interviews to evaluate a candidate's fit with your company.

Crafting a better screening interview

Screening interviews are meant to weed out candidates who are obviously a poor fit. The purpose of a screening interview is simply to decide if a candidate should be scheduled for a longer face-to-face interview.

Chances are your human resources department can handle this step through a phone interview. In fact, I highly recommend using the phone for this interview because it will help them (or you) evaluate the candidate's phone skills.

Your role would be to develop a short set of questions to get at some basic qualifiers. Here are my top 10 questions for screening interviews:

1. What type of position are you looking for?

2. As a salesperson, what are you good at?

3. What do you like most about selling? What do you like the least?

4. On a scale of 1 (low) to 10 (high) how do you think your current/most recent sales manager will rate your contribution to the team when we talk to him or her?

5. Regarding your current (or most recent) sales position:

   a. What were you hired to do?

   b. What were your most outstanding achievements?

   c. What aspect of the position did you find most frustrating?

   d. What were/are your reasons for leaving that position?

6. Do you consider yourself coachable? Why or why not?

7. What kind of work environment do you think best suits your personality? Have you been in a work environment where you just didn't fit in? Why?

8. Since you have decided to make a job change, what criteria are you using to select your next employer?

9. What do you know about our company?

10. What questions can I answer for you?

During the interview, your human resources staff are listening for any obvious reason why a candidate would not be a good fit for the company or the position. By the time they get to the final question, they should have a pretty good idea of whether they want to schedule a longer interview with you.

Better hiring interviews

There's an old saying that the most effective strategy is to "hire the wills, coach the skills." So hiring interviews are essentially a test of how well you can determine whether a candidate has the right wills (attitudes). Your best hires are those that will fit well into your company culture. Tweaking some standard interview questions to dig a little deeper may help to reveal the true talents (or not) of your sales candidates.

Here are some tips:

1. Don't tell the candidate what you're looking for—that is, don't use the descriptors you've just developed that relate to wills, culture, or coachability. Instead, ask open-ended questions.

2. Ask the same question in different conversations, especially questions about sales results, number of months they were over quota, and so on. You want to see if the candidate will give consistent answers.

3. Probe for complete answers and specifics. You want to hear about every aspect of a situation (what exactly was going on, what they or a customer did, how they assessed the situation, what steps they took, and so on).

4. Ask behavioral questions. I favor questions that force candidates to describe their behaviors not just a particular outcome. That gives you more insight into their thought patterns and attitudes. Some examples are shown in Figure 9.

Figure 9: Example Behavioral Questions

Instead of this	Ask this
• What were your outstanding achievements? *(this just asks for outcomes)*	• Give me an example of an outstanding achievement and how you made it happen.
• Do you consider yourself coachable? *(a yes/no question)*	• Tell me about a time when you accepted coaching advice.

Beyond interviews

One technique that I and many other sales managers use is to expose job candidates to a wide variety of people and listen to other opinions. Once when I was hiring a sales rep for a division that I led, I made sure that my office manager (who was a great judge of people), the sales manager of a different division, and our receptionist interacted with the woman throughout the day. Afterward, all three of these people advised me *not* to hire her. Yes, she was enthusiastic, they said, but all of them felt she was too abrasive, too much in-your-face, too obnoxious.

I considered their advice seriously but ultimately decided that there was enough good in this woman to take a chance. But because of their input, I knew her demeanor could be an issue when she dealt with customers. During her first months on the job, therefore, I made sure to observe her behavior and focus my coaching strategies on polishing her interaction skills. And guess what? She turned out to be one of my best hires ever.

Every great sales manager I know has strategies like this that help them get other views of candidates outside the screening and interview interactions. Here are some other favorite strategies I've found helpful.

Job Exposure (Ride-alongs)

In one of my first management positions, I was presented with a sales rep candidate who was the nephew of my company's executive VP of sales (one of three top executives in the firm). The candidate had recently relocated from the Midwest to California and was applying for a sales position in his uncle's firm.

At the time, the company had a four-step hiring process. The nephew made it through the first two steps (screening and interviews) just fine. Step three was what I called "job exposure," where I sent the candidate out in the field for a day with one of my peak performers.

After the ride-along, I decided not to hire the nephew based on what my rep told me, and informed the nephew that he was no longer a candidate. Two days later the phone rang. It was Uncle EVP on the phone.

In a gruff voice, he said, "I understand you decided to pass on my nephew. Can you tell me why?"

Here's what I told him: "I put him out for a field ride with my top rep, Darren. During the day, your nephew told Darren that the real reason he moved to Southern California was that his primary personal ambition was to make it as a professional golfer. He thought he'd have a better chance at achieving that goal here than in the Midwest. I didn't want to hire someone who wouldn't be one hundred percent committed to *our* team and the sales profession."

There was dead silence on the phone for a few moments. Then he gave a little grunt and said, "Good decision, son."

I used this job exposure technique many, many times over the years. It never ceased to amaze me how many things a candidate would tell one of my salespeople that they would never say in a formal interview. Candidates *always* let their guard down! When my rep and a candidate would return to the office at the end of the day, I'd first bring the rep into my office and ask these four questions:

- What questions did the candidate ask you?

- Did the candidate seem at ease with our customers?

- What qualities did you observe in the candidate that would be an asset to our team?

- Did you observe any qualities or habits that could be detrimental to us?

As you can tell from these examples, my hiring process had two "always": I always took responsibility for deciding whether a candidate was a good prospect, but I also always sought out and listened to the advice of others around me, including reps, staff, and other managers.

Do the Diligence

I once hired a sales rep who explained that a gap in his employment history was because he'd signed on with a professional baseball team right after college. He'd made it to the Double-A level (two levels below the majors) but eventually realized that he wasn't going to go any higher. Now, he said, he was leaving baseball behind and seeking to establish a career in sales. I decided to hire him because he had a very competitive spirit, had been part of a team, and seemed to have other qualities that would be appealing in the profession.

By coincidence, about six weeks later my company held an intraoffice softball tournament. Naturally, I put my almost-MLB player at shortstop. In the course of the game he made two errors and bounced numerous throws to first base. Hmm. Suspicions arose.

He didn't last long after that. I decided to dig deeper into his background and discovered several additional inconsistencies besides his nonexistent minor league career. From then on, I made it a habit to study gaps in employment history more carefully and check references!

Making the Call

At the end of a round of interviews with a new hire candidate, ask yourself if you can see that person ranking in the top half of your sales team six months or a year down the road. If not, don't hire the person. Each hiring decision you make will have an impact on your team's culture—and you need the impact to be extremely positive, not negative.

One tip that has repeatedly worked for me is to pick someone slightly *underqualified* for the position. From the candidate's perspective, the job you offer is a *step up* in their career path: more responsibility, more income potential. Seeing the job as an advancement helps create the all-important fire-in-the-belly quality that provides the motivation to learn and succeed.

My father-in-law, Bill, for example, was a very successful sales rep for a large company based in San Francisco for many years. But he started out in finance. How did he make the switch? Long ago, a sales manager asked around the office, "Who is that new employee in the finance department who takes the stairs two at a time?" The manager saw hustle, took action, and the result was a top producer.

If you want to go in this direction, it's important to talk with your human resources department first. You need to make sure that their "minimum standards" for the job are not so high that you have to eliminate the slightly underqualified. When that happens, you lose.

Have a second hiring date

Making a bad hiring decision is something every experienced manager has done. Despite our best efforts, no hiring process is going to be perfect. A new hire won't really know what it's like to work at your company and what is required to succeed until after they've been there a while.

If the mistake costs you three months' time, that's not good. If you don't realize you made a hiring mistake for a year or two, the damage can be catastrophic.

I advise companies to have a standard policy that defines the first 90 to 120 days (and maybe a little longer) as a *trial* period. After that point, the candidate's fit is reevaluated. You will look at the new hire, evaluate their progress, then decide whether to keep or de-hire that new rep. Having a second hiring date in your mind will help you focus on observing how your new salesperson is progressing.

During that trial period, you will want to pay attention to signs that the person is *not* the right fit, such as these:

- Frequently late or absent

- Low enthusiasm

- Quality or quantity of effort drops

- Complaints about the person

- Frequent complaints by the person

- Spending significant work time on non-work interests

- Displays of anger, dissension, or rule breaking

If you observe some of these problems and the new hire doesn't respond to your coaching, cut your losses. You can talk all you want about having high expectations, but your actions speak louder than words. Your current lowest producer is the de facto minimum acceptable standard you have set for your team! Do not let a lousy new hire lower the minimum even further. Act quickly to remove that player from your team. I've said it before and will say it again: Do not tolerate mediocrity!

If none of these kinds of problems appear and the person makes the grade, *then* you can increase your investment in the person's development. Here are a couple of ways you can do that:

- Provide additional training. What skills does the new hire still need the most work on?

- Target some marketing dollars in their territory to generate more leads and give them a boost.

Getting the Right People on Your Bus

No manager sets out to hire someone that ends up not working out. The lost investment of time and energy and the lost opportunity of having a better rep in that territory are just too costly. The secret to better hiring goes back to the Success Profile concept I discussed in Chapter 3. If you have a clear idea of what it takes to be a star player on your team, you'll be in a stronger position to define better job postings and more effectively evaluate candidates. You'll know that looking at both skills and wills (attitudes) can increase the odds of finding a person who will love and grow into the job, stay with your company, and become an important contributor.

Chapter 5

Insert the Customer in Your Sales Process

Every company has a sales process whether or not it's formalized. Ideally, a sales process provides salespeople with a consistent, repeatable path to follow that leads to a higher probability of sales success. It should also give them guidance for creating new customers and growing sales from current customers. Also, when a sales process is well defined, it is easier to educate sales reps and track their performance.

But there's one other element that's key to an optimal sales process, an element that is missing in most companies: the customer! Though many sales organizations think of themselves as customer-focused because they truly care about the customer, their sales process is seller-focused. Further, their systems—sales models, CRM, funnel structure, and pipeline—are set up to track sales rep activities, not customer actions.

Having a sales process that is inwardly focused rather than customer-focused has serious ripple effects in how you lead and manage your team. To help prove this point, I'd like to tell you the tale of two companies.

In company Alpha, the sales managers and sales teams are all dedicated to their jobs. But life in Alpha is often stressful. Actual results often fall short of forecasts; sales people are trying their best, but sales managers find themselves constantly having to urge the reps to "work harder" to make their numbers. Frustration abounds.

Life in company Beta is much better all around. Sure, forecasts are never one hundred percent accurate, but they come much closer than Alpha's do. Sales reps feel very supported by their sales managers, who have an uncanny knack of providing specific, timely advice that helps reps keep more prospects moving through the funnel.

The difference in these companies and their sales success rates is striking. And it all comes down to one key element: how the companies structure their sales process. Alpha is using a very traditional approach where the sales process and CRM are based on the steps of selling (that is, what reps are supposed to do). Beta's sales process and CRM are structured around how their customers buy.

In this chapter, I'm going to use these companies' experiences to demonstrate the differences between a selling-focused and a buying-focused sales process. These differences explain why Alpha keeps fighting the same battles month in and month out while Beta has increasing win rates. And it also explains why Alpha's salespeople hate their CRM system while Beta's reps have discovered that their system helps them close more deals. I hope these two companies' experiences will get you thinking about ways to become more customer- and buying-focused on your sales team.

Staying with Tradition: A Selling-Focused Sales Model

By calling Alpha's sales model seller-focused, I mean it describes what steps a sales rep should take in order to sell: qualifying leads, needs and solution identified, quotation provided, and so on. You know the drill. This is the standard way that most sales models are structured. Alpha's sales model (Model 1) is shown on the left in Figure 10; I've included two other very common sales process models for comparison.

Figure 10: Example Sales Model

Model 1	Model 2	Model 3
• Prospect	• Contact	• Engaging
• Qualify	• Identify needs	• Discovery
• Identify needs	• Demo	• Confirming
• Present	• Trial	• Recommendation
• Proposal/quotation	• Negotiate	• Committing
• Handle objections	• Decision (won/lost)	
• Close		

I want you to think for a moment about the implications of the structure represented by these models. When a salesperson in these organizations enters data into a CRM, the status they report—the data that sales forecasts are based on—reflects primarily **actions salespeople have taken, not what the customer has done**. So the position that a customer occupies within the funnel—"demo" vs. "trial," for instance— only indicates how far a salesperson has progressed in the steps of selling, not how far a customer has progressed in their decision making.

What too few companies realize, however, is that selling activities are an inaccurate metric of progress because sales reps are so often out of sync with customers' views. It's not necessarily that salespeople are doing the wrong things. They could be doing the right things— identifying needs, delivering proposals, doing demonstrations—but at the wrong time in terms of the customer's buying process.

In short, any deal tracking or forecasts based on a selling-focused model are actually based on sales rep intuition not evidence that a prospect is moving forward. And it's this disconnect between "sales rep actions" and "customer actions" that contributes to lost sales and missed forecasts.

Because Alpha uses this kind of selling-oriented model, sales opportunities can seem to be progressing quite nicely *as long as salespeople are doing the sales tasks the model describes.* Alpha never really knows what is going on inside its customers. A rep who has delivered a proposal may be very confident in the deal going through. But neither the sales rep nor sales managers can tell if the prospect is having second thoughts based on new needs or if the rep's proposal didn't effectively contrast their offerings from the competition. Whatever the reason, nobody in Alpha knows something is wrong until the buyer's *next* step fails to happen on time. The prospect suddenly goes radio-silent and Alpha later learns the sure thing was lost.

I want to elaborate on this concept because it's critical to understand why companies with selling-driven process models are almost constantly disappointed with inaccurate forecasts and poor sales results. While it might sound important to know that a rep has delivered a proposal, simply tracking "proposal delivery" doesn't tell you whether the customer has fully defined their needs or if they understand the economic impact if they do nothing. It doesn't tell you if the customer has compared your offering to those of your competitors, or if they have allocated money for some kind of buying decision. It also can't tell you which (if any) steps the customer has completed in their buying process.

In short, if you're using a selling-focused model, you're flying blind in terms of understanding what is happening with your customers. You can't manage or coach something you cannot see.

There is a second, equally important flaw with selling-focused models that I want to point out. The only data that CRMs associated with these kinds of sales models can capture—such as how many calls, appointments, or demos were made—are all *lagging indicators*, data that reflect the near or distant past and not what is currently happening. Therefore, most coaching done by sales managers at Alpha (and any other company with a similar model) is what I characterize as "performance management," where managers evaluate their salespeople after the fact rather than *teach* and *develop* them.

I discussed the problems with performance management in the book's introduction. These data provide no insights into the causes or solutions to problems for specific sales opportunities; they don't help you understand what is going well inside the buyer. So sales managers have little option with an underperforming rep other than to crack the whip and say, "Make more calls!" (Meanwhile, salespeople are thinking, "That's the same advice you gave me last month and it didn't help.")

The importance of knowing why (improving predictability)

While it's possible for many salespeople to do a decent job of selling by following the steps in their company's model, the inability to dive into the reasons a sale did or did not go through makes their job tougher. Without knowing the *why*, it's difficult to replicate the success in one deal to the *next*, or to say that because one deal fell through another like it will too. That means deals are more unpredictable.

Predictability is in many ways as important as driving sales growth. Companies and investors stake valuation on predictability; comp plans and quotas are built on predictability. And ultimately, sales reps and managers will be judged on both sales growth and predictability (sales forecast accuracy). If there is sales growth that was not predicted, the reps are often suspected of "sandbagging"—not booking sales one month to help them qualify for the next month's incentive or exceed the next month's quota. The bosses see a big leap in sales and then raise quotas accordingly.

Having a buying-focused sales model increases predictability and hence funnel accuracy.

A More Effective Approach: Buying-Focused Models

A few years ago, sales executives at Beta became alarmed about poor user adoption of their CRM system. Salespeople were not entering information in a timely manner, so the accuracy of the information being recorded was questionable. Not good.

Why do many sales reps reject CRM? The top reasons include concerns about a perceived loss of confidentiality/control of data, the time required to input data, and managers using the CRM system as a policing tool. Seasoned salespeople may also have the attitude that they "own" their contacts and they don't want to share what they see as a valuable resource that contributes to their success (and paycheck!).

Recognizing these realities, Beta decided that simply providing more training on the CRM system wasn't the answer. Its sales force needed to be more motivated to use the system, which would happen only if they thought doing so would help them improve results. What would help salespeople improve results? **A better understanding of customer buying and more insights into what might be going wrong inside a prospective opportunity.** To get that kind of knowledge, Beta would have to revamp its sales model into something that was much more rooted in customer buying behavior than the steps of selling.

To help Beta understand this concept, I introduced them to the **buy-learning model** (Figure 11) that I've used since 1996.[14] The label indicates that customers are *learning* at each step along the way to making a purchase—so selling is really a task of providing customers with the right information at the right time so they can move from one step of buying to another.

---

14   The key message of my first book, *Getting Into Your Customer's Head* (Times Business Books, 1996), was that understanding the buying process is where effective selling should start.

Figure 11: Typical Buying Process

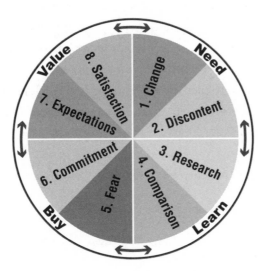

For a sales team, most often the focus is on Steps 1 to 6, which cover everything from the customer's first inkling that change might be necessary to a commitment to make a purchase. Here is a quick overview of what is happening inside a customer at each of these steps:

1. **Change**: Becomes aware of a potential issue and receptive to alternatives and remedies

2. **Discontent**: Conducts problem analysis and economic analysis; develops "solution vision"

3. **Research**: Learns from supplier(s) how vision could be implemented; defines formal and informal decision criteria; prepares a formal or informal RFP

4. **Comparison**: Establishes short list; analyzes proposals; attends demos

5. **Fear**: Tests proof of concept; checks references

6. **Commitment**: Negotiates terms and conditions

Your company may have or want to develop its own model, but this sequence is what I'll be referring to in the rest of this chapter.

Having a model is essential, but not enough. The real value comes in what you should do next to make it actionable. That work involves defining what **actions** you would see a customer take as they move through each of the buying steps. Here are some customer buying actions that Beta sales reps observed (listed in no particular order):

- Agree to an appointment.

- Enable access to other decision makers.

- Articulate buying criteria.

- Share inside information about problems and needs.

- Ask for terms.

- Share performance data (the results they've seen).

- Share their concerns with us.

- Call our references.

- Attend a presentation and review our proposal.

- Visit one of our branch offices or a customer site.

- Provide referrals.

The match between the buying steps and these customer actions is shown in Figure 12.

Figure 12: Customer Actions

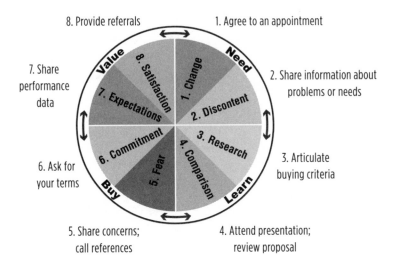

8. Provide referrals   1. Agree to an appointment

7. Share
performance
data

2. Share information about
problems or needs

6. Ask for
your terms

3. Articulate
buying criteria

5. Share concerns;   4. Attend presentation;
call references   review proposal

You can use the knowledge of your customers' buying process in a number of different ways to help your sales reps improve their effectiveness. Here are three specific applications that Beta had for a buying-focused model:

1. Sales playbook

2. CRM systems

3. Funnels and forecasting

A More Effective Sales Playbook

I'm a big fan of having a **sales playbook** that documents the general sales process you want reps to use and provides examples of best practices for a variety of specific situations, such as selling different types of products or services to specific types of decision makers. Playbooks also include job aids, scripts, sample proposals, planners to be used at each step of selling, and so on. The content should be customized to your company's needs and reflect your knowledge of the customer's buying process, including the steps they take in buying.

I say "book," but a playbook could be a physical binder or knowledge embedded in your CRM or other online system. Either way, you want reps to be able to sort or find information on specific decision makers they encounter, the product and solution types you offer, and so on.

Company Beta developed this kind of playbook around its new buying-focused sales model. They then made sure it was readily accessible via a virtual interface. That way, team members could quickly and easily find answers to questions such as these:

- Which success stories should I use to begin a meeting with a specific type of decision maker, based on where that person is in the buying process?

- What problems does this decision maker have that our product or service can solve?

- What questions should I ask to develop those problems into explicit customer needs?

- What will each decision maker's buying criteria likely be?

- What will our competitors offer this decision maker, and what are their strengths and weaknesses against us?

- Where can I see our company's most effective sales proposals and written sales correspondence?

- What doubts and concerns will I need to overcome in order to win?

Using a playbook to develop role-plays

Unless your company already has a buying-focused sales model, learning to think that way represents a big shift to salespeople. To become proficient and confident in buying-focused selling, reps must practice determining where a customer is in their buying process, and work on problem-solving skills and questioning techniques. Surely you would rather they gain this practice through role-playing with you than when dealing with a customer! If you have your company's buying-focused sales process baked into the playbook, you have a ready source for developing role-playing scenarios that you can run with your reps. Add in a flexibility twist by creating scenarios based on unusual events from the past or asking unexpected questions.

A Buying-Focused CRM

Remember that the starting point for Beta was wanting to increase the CRM system usage rate among sales reps. Redefining their model to be more buying-focused was a good start; doing a sales playbook was the next step. Lastly, I told them they needed to incorporate knowledge of customer buying and effective selling strategies into their CRM tool. The ideal CRM system combines your sales steps with the buying steps of customers and adds the features of a sales playbook (such as access to templates and sample scripts).

An example of what I described for Beta is shown in Figure 13. This figure shows several screen captures from a CRM tool into which **exit criteria** have been embedded.

Figure 13: Buying-Focused CRM Sales Playbook

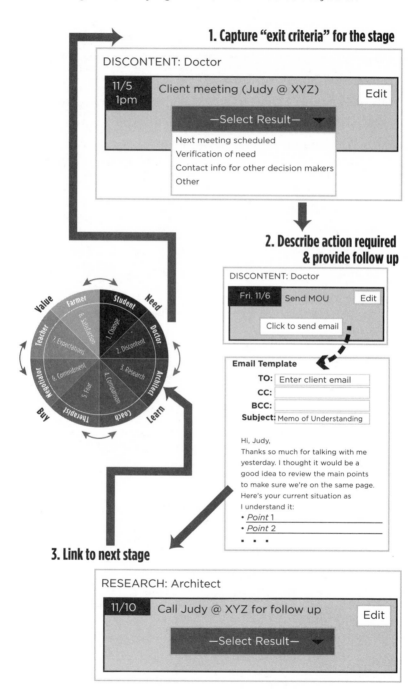

Exit criteria are the specific actions that customers take that indicate they are moving from one step of buying to the next. I've added the buying wheel image so you can see how using Beta's CRM tool now prompts salespeople to do the things that will help customers complete those transitions between buying steps more quickly (the example shows the move from the Discontent step to the Research step).

Simply restructuring the CRM tool around a buying-focused model is not enough, however, to make it attractive to sales reps. If you want it to be truly useful, you need to embed your sales playbook into it, as well. An example of this is shown in Figure 14. With a few clicks, sales reps can call up templates, hints, and even scripts to help them prepare for a meeting with a customer.

Figure 14: Sales Playbook Elements of CRM

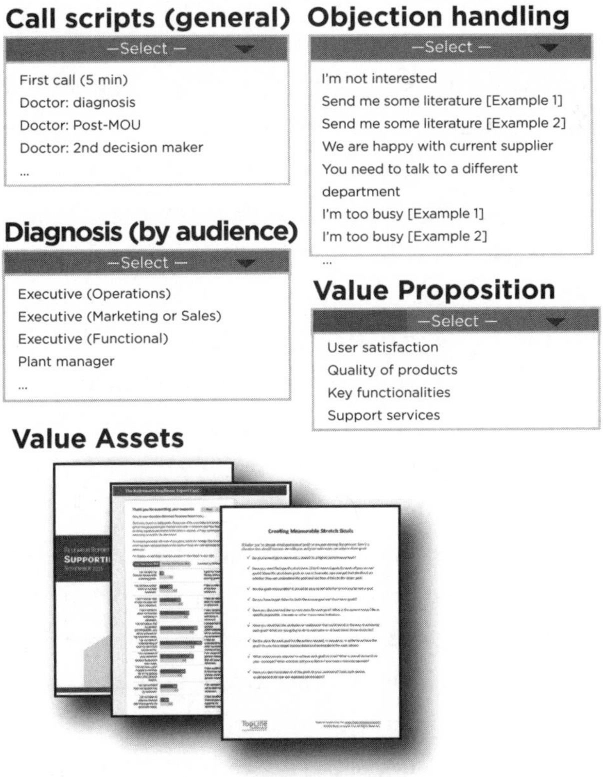

Call scripts (general)

—Select —

First call (5 min)
Doctor: diagnosis
Doctor: Post-MOU
Doctor: 2nd decision maker
...

Objection handling

—Select —

I'm not interested
Send me some literature [Example 1]
Send me some literature [Example 2]
We are happy with current supplier
You need to talk to a different department
I'm too busy [Example 1]
I'm too busy [Example 2]
...

Diagnosis (by audience)

—Select —

Executive (Operations)
Executive (Marketing or Sales)
Executive (Functional)
Plant manager
...

Value Proposition

—Select —

User satisfaction
Quality of products
Key functionalities
Support services

Value Assets

Greater visibility into opportunity status

With a buying-focused process and CRM system in place, Beta's sales managers now have **greater visibility** into the status and progress for each opportunity, which helps them identify specific problems at each stage of the sales process. This helps them provide more timely and tailored coaching to reps on general sales skills and opportunity management. It also enables more accurate forecasting, as I'll discuss next.

The Improved Predictability of a Buying-Focused Funnel

Let's quickly review the purpose of a sales funnel. You, the manager, want to be able to forecast sales so you can submit numbers that will be used in revenue estimates for planning and budgeting purposes. For a salesperson, a sales funnel is supposed to help them move opportunities toward a successful conclusion (making the sale), so they can predict their income both near- and long-term.

In any sales funnel, there should be many more opportunities in the top half (early steps) of the funnel than there are in the bottom half, usually by a factor of at least 3 to 1. Any deviation from that is cause for concern. For example, if a funnel has 50 percent of the opportunities in the bottom half and 50 percent in the top half, a rep's near-term sales prospects are good but longer-term sales are iffy. So the rep needs to do more prospecting *now* to get more opportunities in the top of the funnel.

In this way, a funnel (and the associated processes a company has in place) that is working correctly helps salespeople make better decisions about how to spend their time—that is, what specific actions they should take next to move deals forward. That prevents sales reps from riding a roller coaster: hero one month, zero the next.

The knowledge of customer buying and exit criteria helps in another way. As we all know, every sales funnel leaks—that's why it looks like a funnel instead of a straight chute! And because of the very nature of buying and selling, there will never be a sales funnel that doesn't leak (Figure 15).

Figure 15: Why does your funnel leak?

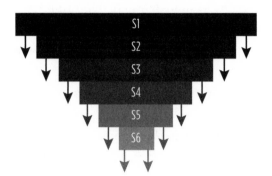

When you create a buying-focused funnel, you can identify potential leaks much sooner and work to plug them. That's because the exit criteria create places all along the buying process—from the very beginning to the end—where you can test the customer's commitment to moving forward and evaluate the pace of their buying process. For example, suppose a rep says, "I have some references that I'd like you to contact now so that you'll have relevant insight into the positive impact our solution provides." It makes a big difference whether the prospect says, "Great! We'd like to hear about other companies' experiences," or "We're not at that stage yet. I'll let you know when to send it over."

Or on another opportunity, a rep says, "I'd like you to have your legal department review our user's license." Does the customer give the rep the appropriate contact information, or do they say, "Well, we're not really ready for that at this time because we need a few more executives to sign off on this general concept first"?

Depending on these answers, you and your sales rep will know whether a deal is on pace to close as forecasted or if it has stalled. Most importantly, if the warning signals appear while the salesperson is still engaged with the customer, the rep can talk with the customer and explore reasons why there is a problem, and thus be in a better position to figure out a way to get the deal back on track. Compare that to a traditional funnel where the rep doesn't know it's too late until after the customer has decided to go in another direction.

Understanding more quickly where opportunities are leaking and why is crucial for effective coaching, and it's crucial for your marketing department to know, as well. From an individual standpoint, understanding the cause of a leak can help a rep improve their skills. And it changes the nature of coaching conversations, as I'll discuss in Chapter 9.

From a team perspective, the reasons may lead to new priorities for coaching or training. For example, if a high proportion of opportunities are leaking in the buyer's Discontent phase, perhaps your salespeople need more training on diagnostic questioning or you may need to shift your selling strategies to incorporate a more formal cost/benefit analysis. Or maybe having your marketing department create more customer success stories will help demonstrate a wider range of benefits than prospects are thinking about originally.

Funnels, CRMs, and forecasting

Combining a buying-focused CRM and playbook with a sales funnel can benefit a company when it comes to forecasting. Traditionally, companies attach a probability to each phase of the funnel. For example, a company may determine that an opportunity in the proposal phase has a 50 percent probability of closing. Personally, I'm never sure what that means. That a sales rep has a 50 percent probability of finishing their sales process? Or that even if they do everything right from then on, the opportunity only has a 50 percent chance of ending in a sale?

In any case, the forecasted numbers in a traditional system, as you now realize, are based on sales rep intuition as much as anything else. With a buying-focused funnel, you can be much more precise about predictions and the basis for assigning various probabilities.

An example of what I mean is shown in Figure 16. The target percentages here are based on overall sales team numbers from past performances. The actual and stage completion are for a specific deal being pursued by a specific rep. Here, the company knows that of all the opportunities that make it into Stage 2: Discontent, 35 percent of them move on to Stage 3: Research. On this deal, the rep completed only 60 percent of the recommended tasks (based on buy-learning insights and customer actions) in the embedded playbook. Therefore, the actual probability that this opportunity will move from Stage 2 to Stage 3 is only 20 percent (vs. the target of 35 percent).

Figure 16: Example CRM Scoring

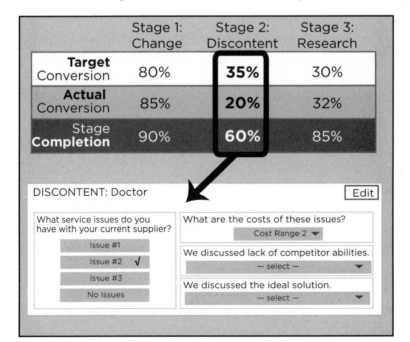

This kind of system gives sales reps immediate feedback on the probability of conversion for each opportunity at each step of the funnel—and these steps are all linked to the customer actions that have been defined as exit criteria. It's like having an automated sales coach. Furthermore, each rep can be scored on how well they complete each step of selling—with documentation on why a particular score is assigned. That increases **rep accountability**, something that many companies are interested in these days. Also, it imposes better process compliance within the team.

Optimism, but verified!

One of sales managers' biggest frustrations is reps who don't close forecasted deals. Salespeople are optimists at heart, and it's easy to believe their rosy forecasts, especially when they've done everything described in your sales funnel or CRM system. But as a sales manager, you have to temper the salesperson's enthusiasm by finding ways to verify their optimism. Having a buying-focused sales model and funnel is one way to do that.

When you connect customer commitments to your funnel, you compel your salespeople to become more customer-focused. If a rep forecasts that an opportunity is going to close in the near future, you can ask, "What actions has the customer taken that led you to that projection?" Compare their answers to the funnel exit criteria and you'll get more accurate forecasts of buying decisions.

Also, in many cases, the decision to buy represents a major commitment from the customer. Rather than expect that commitment to come all at once, surely it makes sense to have your salespeople ask for much less significant commitments along the way—such as agreeing to meetings, sharing information, and so on. If the customer doesn't agree to or follow through on the minor things, it's unlikely they will come through at the end with a major commitment.

The Benefits of a Buying Focus

Here are four ways in which Beta benefited from making this switch in its sales funnel and using customer actions as exit criteria that defined the transitions from one stage of the funnel to the next:

1. The sales reps (and the company as a whole) have truly become more customer-focused. My second book, *Slow Down, Sell Faster*,[15] expanded on the buying-focused concept by observing that the biggest mistake salespeople make is that they sell too fast. They move through the steps of their sales process without thinking about where the customer is in their buying process—what I refer to as the "show up and throw up" syndrome. They're out of sync with the customer. Having a buying-focused sales funnel helps salespeople break this bad habit and do a better job of matching their sales steps to customer buying (that is, getting in sync with customers).

2. Sales reps have more confidence in their process. Being a sales rep in Beta is more straightforward than it is in Alpha. The

---

15   Kevin Davis, *Slow Down, Sell Faster: Understand Your Customer's Buying Process and Maximize Your Sales* (AMACOM Books, 2011).

Beta reps know, based on what has become a "buying funnel" (vs. a sales funnel), what specific actions they need to
get customers to take to keep them moving forward. Before
any meeting or call, reps know to ask, "What specific action
do I want my prospect to take afterward?" That way, every
conversation with a customer is focused on a specific go-forward customer action linked to the exit criteria. The better a
sales rep becomes at having customers complete the exit criteria, the smoother and more predictable the buying funnel
(and sales process) becomes. Take, for example, doing a demo.
Let's suppose that Beta has decided to do its demos early in
the sales process to stimulate prospect interest. So the kind of
go-forward actions a rep might seek from the prospect include
referral to another decision maker, commitment to perform a
workflow analysis, or sharing of inside information not typically shared unless the customer is fairly serious about the
solution concept they're seeing.

3. Sales managers are more effective. A sales VP at Beta recently
   described it this way: "I wanted to have these customer milestones spelled out so my sales managers could be more effective in working with their reps. Now, they can sit down with
   a rep and discuss what steps each prospect has and hasn't
   taken. Then they can talk with the rep very specifically about
   what they need to do to prepare themselves to get that client
   through the next milestone."

4. Sales forecasts are more accurate. Salespeople and sales managers have more knowledge about what a customer or prospect
   is doing (or not doing), and what things the rep has or has not
   completed. This helps them be more realistic when gauging
   the likelihood of success.

Because of these benefits—all of which help salespeople sell more—Beta had no problem achieving its original goal of getting sales reps to use the CRM tool more diligently. Ultimately, the conversion to a buying-focused process allowed Beta sales managers to be more effective in coaching reps and helping their teams close more opportunities.

Obviously, companies can survive with a selling-focused sales process since that's how most models are structured today. If your company falls into that category, though, I hope that Beta's experience has convinced you it's time to rethink that process. I'm not promising that life will all be rosy, but I do guarantee that you will experience far fewer of the headaches that come from neglecting to consider customer behaviors as you manage a sales process. By getting your team focused on customer buying behaviors, both your time and your reps' time can be used to much greater effect.

Priority #1:
Coach and Develop
Your Team

Overview

Ronald Brown, author of *From Selling to Managing*, writes that "good sales management is the ability to get people of ordinary ability to perform at extraordinary levels."[16] Certainly we can all agree with Mr. Brown's concept here. But the question is, how do you actually do that?

A few clues can be found in research on sales coaching conducted in 2014–15 by the Sales Management Association.[17] One aspect of the study involved having sales managers rank 13 topics in order of how often they discussed those topics in coaching conversations. "Identifying skill deficiencies" was ranked way down at #12! It fell well behind topics like "advancing a sales opportunity" and "crafting proposals" and even below the 11th-ranked item, "instruction on administrative processes." So sales managers spent more time making sure their people know how to fill out an expense reimbursement form than improving their sales skills!

In the same study, the researchers looked into the relationship between each of the 13 topics and the organization's revenue growth. Guess what ranked first in terms of having a positive influence on revenue? You guessed it! "Identifying skill deficiencies."

---

16   Ronald Brown, *From Selling to Managing: Guidelines for the First-time Sales Manager* (AMACOM, 1990), p. 5.

17 "Research Report: Supporting Sales Coaching." Sales Management Association. November 2015.

This research reinforced my observation that many sales managers *think* they're having coaching conversations with salespeople—but they're not. At least they're not having conversations that contribute to reps' personal development and growth. They may be working with a rep on closing a deal or crafting a specific proposal, but that is not the same as coaching a rep on developing skills that will help them improve their overall rate of success—which is what Priority #1 should be for sales managers.

Effective developmental coaching, therefore, is using your time wisely to fill in the "skill deficiencies"—to which I would add correcting "will deficiencies," as well. By proactively identifying skill and will deficiencies, rather than waiting until a problem becomes too large to ignore, sales managers can more effectively coach their team.

The chapters in this part of the book are focused on how to do more—and more effective—developmental coaching while at the same time continuing to drive improved results.

Chapter 6: Become a More Strategic Coach discusses sales mindsets that can prevent sales managers from using their coaching time most effectively and presents alternative leadership strategies.

Chapter 7: Commit to Consistent Coaching provides a new mental model to help you think differently about all the coaching you do.

Chapter 8: Motivate the Demotivated focuses specifically on willingness and motivation and what you as a coach can do to motivate all of your reps to higher levels of performance.

Chapter 9: Increase Win Rates with Buying-Cycle Coaching picks up on the buying-focused sales process discussion in Chapter 5 and shows how you can make your coaching discussions more customer-focused. By helping reps better understand a sale from the customer's perspective, you're giving them the skills they need to drive bigger sales and increase their win rates.

Chapter 6

Become a More Strategic Coach

I'd been managing a single sales team for two years at the point that I was transferred to a different office and put into a general manager position. It was, for me, a big promotion. My responsibility included oversight of two sales teams, plus field service and office admin/support. Like any new manager, I was determined to start off on the right foot.

The general manager before me had left a bit of a mess as far as the sales teams were concerned. He had been something of an arrogant micromanager, and one of his sales managers had quit about six months prior. Then the general manager was de-hired and I was brought in.

My new boss told me that I needed to focus my attention first on getting the two sales teams back on track. My plan for my first hundred days included spending about 80 percent of my time working in the field with salespeople. I needed to observe and assess our people prior to making any personnel decisions.

The good news was that there were a few successful salespeople, a small nucleus that I could build a team around. The bad news was that the micromanaging predecessor had been a "desk jockey," and the salespeople were in bad need of direct sales coaching.

To help me get a general sense of one team's status, after doing some initial ride-alongs, I rated each rep on their overall skill and will levels using a scale of 1 (low) to 5 (high).[18] You can see the results in Table D. The people in this scenario are all real, though obviously I have disguised their identities.

Table D: Example Sales Team

Name	Skill	Will
Ann T. Oxidant	5	5
Clare Voyant	2	3
Sal Monella	3	5
Willy Sellmore	2	2
Carlotta Tendant	5	2
Al Fresco	4	4

Knowing that Ann (first row, best ratings) would hit her numbers without help from me, I subsequently spent much of my coaching time through the rest of those first hundred days doing ride-alongs with people like Willy Sellmore, whose name reflects the question in my brain every time I talked with him—*will he sell more?* On those rides, I heard a lot of excuses from Willy, Sal, and Clare, all of whom had been on the job less than 12 months, about why their sales numbers were low: "Our product line sucks." . . . "Our service department is slow." . . . "Our pricing is too high." . . . "Our competition is discounting."

If you had a team like this, what would you do first? What

18   In Chapter 3, I talked about the helpfulness of rating reps on individual skills and wills to help identify development needs. This situation was different in that I just wanted to see where the team stood overall.

strategies would you employ? Would you work most with Willy and Clare? Focus your time on helping Ann and Al close their big deals?

Before I discuss what I ended up doing with this team, let me first provide a little background on effective coaching strategies. I'll then use the team ratings table to illustrate how those strategies work out in real life, and finally summarize some principles for triaging your valuable coaching time.

Strategic Coaching

When it comes to coaching, most sales managers have natural instincts to either **rescue the worst players** (because obviously they need the most help) or **gravitate to the best players** (because they will likely have the biggest, most exciting deal opportunities).

If either of these sounds like you, the results of a study reported in the *Harvard Business Review*[19] might come as a surprise.

> In research involving thousands of reps, we found that coaching—even world-class coaching—has a marginal impact on either the weakest or the strongest performers in the sales organization. You'd think that coaching the lowest performers would pay off because they have nowhere to go but up. Actually, that's often not true, particularly for the bottom 10 percent. These reps, we've found, are less likely to be underperformers who can improve, and more likely to be a bad fit for the role altogether. That's not really something coaching can fix. It's likely a different kind of conversation altogether (often involving HR).

---

19 Matthew Dixon and Brent Adamson, "HBR Blog: The Dirty Secret of Effective Sales Coaching," *Harvard Business Review.* January 31, 2011. https://hbr.org/2011/01/the-dirty-secret-of-effective

Likewise, star-performing reps show virtually no performance improvement due to coaching either. While our research shows that there are some important retention benefits from coaching your high performers, it would be nice to think that great coaching (especially from former high performers) makes your stars just a little more stellar. But that's just not the case.

Our conclusion? The real payoff from good coaching lies among the middle 60 percent—your core performers.

That's right. Your biggest payoff from coaching will come from working with the people you might think of as your "B" players. Your mindset needs to be focusing your one-on-one coaching time on the people with the **biggest potential**, not those with the biggest problems or biggest deals. I call these people the **high-payoff coaching candidates**. Spending time with the high-potential people will have a much bigger impact on your team's performance. It is also a way to give your "A" players more competition!

That's why I suggest doing one more tweak to the rating approach by looking at overall **competency** (skill) and **coachability** (will) ratings for your reps (Figure 17), perhaps once or twice every six months.

Figure 17: Competency & Coachability Ratings

	Sales Competency	Coachability
Name 1		
Name 2		
Name 3		
Name 4		
Name 5		

There are several uses for this table. You can, for instance, sort everyone in rank order from highest to lowest so you have a semi-objective way of identifying your best and worst performers. You can use these ratings to identify the coaching needs for each rep. Do they just not have the skill or knowledge to do a better job, or do they know what to do but lack the will or attitude to make themselves successful? Have they improved in the last few months or are they stagnating?

More specifically, you can use the table to identify the high-payoff coaching candidates—the people who have low to moderate skill but high will (or coachability), and therefore where your one-on-one coaching time will have the biggest impact. Table E, for example, is the sales team I referenced earlier, this time with Sal Monella highlighted. At the time, he had only a moderate skill level but was very eager to learn, so I knew that devoting one-on-one coaching time to him would likely be high payoff.

Table E: High-Payoff Coaching Candidate on My Sales Team

Name	Skill	Will
Ann T. Oxidant	5	5
Clare Voyant	2	3
Sal Monella	3	5
Willy Sellmore	2	2
Carlotta Tendant	5	2
Al Fresco	4	4

As an aside, I encourage you to take good notes on *why* you're giving people specific numbers. First and foremost, these notes will be important in determining what actions you want to take with a sales rep; that is, what does each person need to improve to get better in their ratings? You can also use the notes when you have one-on-one coaching discussions with reps, a subject I address at length later in the book. Most reps I know are eager to get helpful feedback (though they don't relish after-the-fact criticism that doesn't help them improve). So use your notes to talk about specifics with your reps and share your ideas on what each person needs to get better.

Second, the notes will reveal what your approach to coaching has been (what do you pay attention to? how have you been assessing your people? are you being a developmental coach or a performance manager?). Now that you have a general sense of rating your team, I want to pick up a theme from Chapter 1 on how sales instincts can work to the detriment of effective leadership.

A report card on YOU!

By rating your salespeople, what you've really done is given yourself a grade in terms of *your effectiveness as a sales coach.* If there are common problems across the team, what do you have to do to get better so that your team can get better?

The Ballad of Willy Sellmore (or why it's a bad idea to "never give up")

Winston Churchill, the great British leader during World War II, was widely revered for being an inspirational figure during some very difficult times. British citizens heard the message to "never give up" even during the darkest days of the war.

That kind of tenacity is very valuable in salespeople; it makes them persist and win more deals. But when present in a sales manager, a potentially damaging effect occurs when we hang on to low producers too long. We don't want to give up on people we hire, even if they turn out to be a poor performer.

As I mentioned in Chapter 4, nearly every sales manager I meet agrees that there is someone on the team that in hindsight they would not have hired. And they've often known the person was a bad fit for many months if not years. In other words, the typical sales manager is holding on to a Willy Sellmore, the one rep they know is not *and never will be* a good fit for the team.

What I want you to do is think a little more deeply about what impact this has on your team.

Take my inspired-by-reality sales team, for example. When presented with this team's ratings (Table F), most managers tell me they would focus a lot of coaching time on Willy and Clare. But as the research I just presented demonstrates, that is a low-impact strategy.

Table F: What to Do with a Poor Performer?

Name	Skill	Will
Ann T. Oxidant	5	5
Clare Voyant	2	3
Sal Monella	3	5
Willy Sellmore	2	2
Carlotta Tendant	5	2
Al Fresco	4	4

Think of it this way: What label does Clare Voyant give to Willy Sellmore? The answer is "job security." As long as Willy is allowed to remain on the team, even though he has the lowest ratings (and hence the worst sales numbers), Clare can be pretty sure she will not be the next person to be fired! She is not thinking about success and achievement; she is thinking, "I've just got to be a *little bit* better than Willy." And as a sales manager, you have to ask yourself if that is an acceptable standard of performance for your sales team.

What should you do instead? Generally, I recommend doing *group* coaching on skills and wills (instead of one-on-one). But if nothing changes, then you should **cut your losses** sooner rather than later. Recent research shows just what a terrible mistake it is to keep someone with a poor attitude on a team: Just one bad apple on a team can reduce the overall team performance by 30 percent.[20]

Knowing what I know now, for example, I would have let Willy Sellmore go ("de-hired" him, in the modern jargon) far earlier than I did in reality. Allowing him to stay on the team set a bad example for everyone and gave the others a safety cushion that removed an incentive for them to improve.

You are responsible for keeping your salespeople focused on the behaviors you need them to perform to achieve sales success. You are responsible for making sure your team members aspire to high standards. If you see something happening that is not successful, you must address the issue now.

Finding the Right Balance with Top Performers

I know I just told you that working with your "B players" should be a top priority and the research I cited said there was little impact from working with top performers. And earlier in the book I advised against falling victim to the instinct to chase big deals.

20   For example, see Robert Sutton's "How a Few Bad Apples Ruin Everything," *The Wall Street Journal* (October 24, 2011), which cites a number of studies.

Yet at the same time, I don't think any sales manager should leave their "A players" alone entirely, for two reasons.

First, there's no such thing as perfection in our profession any more than there is in any other profession. Top producers often got into selling so they could have a lot of independence in how they work. They don't usually seek help, especially if good results provide validation that they are doing things right. Their sales managers—always former top sales performers themselves—tacitly agree with that interpretation. The underlying assumption is that top performers are as good as they can get.

But one thing we know about success is that it can blind us to opportunities to get even better. In his 2007 book *The Science of Success*,[21] Charles Koch, CEO of Koch Industries, writes, "Given human nature, we tend to become complacent, self-protective, and less innovative as we become successful. It is often more difficult to overcome success than adversity."

Be a role model for seeking and accepting feedback

I recently saw a comment on a management blog from a top performer who wrote that he'd be leery of accepting advice from managers who thought they were always right. He would be more likely to seek out and accept advice from a manager if that manager had asked *him* for input on how to improve. So don't try to wrap yourself in an aura of perfection. If you are willing to learn how to get better, so will your top performers.

---

21 Charles G. Koch, *The Science of Success: How Market-based Management Built the World's Largest Private Company* (Wiley, 2007).

Second, your top performers can set the tone for your team around both skills and will. If *they* have the attitude of always striving to get better, their success example will provide inspiration for the entire sales team.

With that in mind, there are two particular coaching strategies that I think are good for keeping your top performers at the peak of their game.

1. Consistently enforce standards

The book *Wooden*,[22] the autobiography of John Wooden (legendary UCLA basketball coach), has over 200 brief anecdotes from Wooden's life. One that I find informative involves Wooden and Bill Walton, the team's All-American star player. At the time, there was a rule banning facial hair for players on UCLA's team. After a 10-day break, Walton came to practice with a beard. Coach Wooden asked him if he was forgetting something.

Walton: "Coach, if you mean the beard, I think I should be allowed to wear it. It's my right."

Wooden: "Do you believe in that strongly, Bill?"

Walton: "Yes, coach, I do. Very much."

Wooden: "Bill, I have great respect for individuals who stand up for those things in which they believe. I really do. And the team is going to miss you."

Bill went into the locker room and shaved off his beard.

Wooden writes, "There were no hard feelings. . . . I wasn't angry and Walton wasn't mad at me. He understood that the choice was between his own desires and the good of the team. I think if I had given in to him I would have lost control not only of Bill but of his teammates."

To me, the most important lesson from this story is that the team

---

22 John Wooden (with Steve Jamison), *Wooden: A Lifetime of Observations and Reflections On and Off the Court* (Contemporary Books, 1997).

had standards that were *equally enforced* no matter the status of the player. You must have the same attitude.

2. Develop another Bell Cow

In my original team, Ann T. Oxidant served as a pretty good Bell Cow—someone who is a leader and whom others follow and emulate. But because the only other top seller, Carlotta, had such a poor attitude, Ann didn't have much competition—and I always like having a little pressure on my top performers. The best sales teams I have ever been a part of had competition at the top; there was more than one peak performer and they were competing with each other, way above sales quota.

None of the other original team members could step into that same Bell Cow role, however, or they were unwilling to do so (Carlotta). So after I de-hired Willy Sellmore, I hired Ivan Inkling, who, as you can see (Table G), rated very high on willingness even though his skill set was low.

Table G: Who Is Ann's Competition?

Name	Skill	Will
Ann T. Oxidant	5	5
Clare Voyant	2	3
Sal Monella	3	5
Carlotta Tendant	5	2
Al Fresco	4	4
Ivan Inkling	2	5

I devoted a lot of coaching time to Ivan, and he learned very quickly, putting in a lot of hard work. Soon, he was second only to Ann in both his ratings, outdistancing even Sal (the other high-payoff coaching candidate). That not only gave Ann some competition but motivated Carlotta to change her attitude as well!

This strategy of developing team leaders and Bell Cows is tried and true. Coaches know that leadership is tied not only to how long a player has been around, but also to how that person produces and how he or she interacts with others on the team. Salespeople take their cues from another peer, not management.

Your responsibility is to make sure that the person seen by your team as their role model is a positive role model, not a negative one. You can find an example of this in the book[23] and movie *Moneyball*, the story of how Oakland Athletics general manager Billy Beane (played by Brad Pitt in the movie) turned around the team's seasons-long losing streak to set an American League record by winning 20 consecutive games during the 2002 baseball season.

There's a scene in the movie where Beane approaches one of his experienced players, David Justice, who was practicing alone in the batting cage. Up to this point, Justice had been more of a lone wolf, perhaps bordering on what I'd call a prima donna. Beane says, "David, I need you to step up and become more of a leader of this team. Make an example for the younger players. Check in with them, see how they're doing and help them more." Beane was asking Justice to become his team's Bell Cow. Justice proceeded to do what Beane asked, and in doing so helped propel the team on a record-setting roll.

Look at your own team right now and figure out who has the greatest potential to be developed into a Bell Cow.[24]

23 Michael Lewis, *Moneyball: The Art of Winning an Unfair Game* (W.W. Norton & Co., 2004).

24 Whenever I discuss this topic in a seminar, often someone brings up the classic "Cow Bell" skit from *Saturday Night Live!*, starring Will Ferrell, Christopher Walken, and Jimmy Fallon. The lesson from that skit is quite different, which I discussed in a blog post: http://toplineleadership.com/sales-team-need-cowbell-2

Triaging Your Coaching Time

The popularity of TV medical dramas has made the concept of **triage** more widely known in the public. The generic meaning of "triage" is to sort or sift items so you can assign priorities and resources to projects or people. That's what I want you to do with your team; sort your team into different categories based on what type of coaching intervention will represent the best use of your time.

I've summarized my approach to triaging a sales team in Table H. The table recaps the three strategies previously discussed in this chapter (working with high-payoff candidates, dealing with poor performers like Willy, and creating Bell Cows), and includes a fourth category, the troubled talent. This category represents someone who was once a good producer, but whose results have fallen off and they show no motivation to improve. Dealing with low willingness is the subject of Chapter 8, so you'll find more details there about how to deal with that kind of rep.

What about new hires?

If you've done a good job of hiring (see Chapter 4), a new rep should be low to moderate in skill level, but hopefully very high in willingness (if not, why did you hire that person?). All new hires deserve your time and attention. Make sure they get the training and coaching they need to become quickly integrated and profitable. Perhaps after the "second hiring date" (see p. 86), you could start to include them in the table of ratings with the rest of your team.

The Strategy of Effective Coaching

The main point of this chapter is that coaching time is a resource that needs to be managed. It needs to be allocated carefully according to your priorities. Unfortunately, the reps who are the most in need of you are probably not the reps you should be spending most of your time with. In fact, quite possibly the team members who are the least demanding of your time and attention are the ones who would benefit the most from your coaching. So if you just follow your instincts—whether it's to work with top performers or bottom performers—you will not be using your coaching time most effectively. However, while the players on your team won't all need the same kind or amount of coaching, everyone will need *some* attention from you.

Keep in mind that the initial goal here is to develop the players on your team, not punish or reprimand them. A great sales manager is one who gives every person a chance to improve, but does not tolerate poor or mediocre results for too long.

Table H: Triage Strategies

Category	Skill	Will	Description	Development strategy
The high-pay-off coaching candidates	Lo / mod	Hi	Persons of low to moderate skill but who are very coachable.	Use most of your one-on-one time with this group. Their willingness to learn means they are more likely to listen to and implement your advice.
Your best Bell Cow(s)	Hi	Hi	The person with the highest ratings in both categories. Can serve as a role model for the team.	Engage this person in becoming a mentor and role model for the team. Ask them to help develop a playbook or other best practices documents.
The troubled talent	Hi	Lo	A person who has a lot of skill but either never had or has lost their will to support the team or the company.	One-on-one coaching on skills won't work, so the focus has to be on motivation and engagement. An example conversation with someone in this category is shown in Chapter 8.
A problem performer	Lo	Lo	A person who has received adequate training and coaching but has a poor attitude.	The impact of improvements will likely be minimal in terms of your team's achievement. You don't want to ignore these reps (every employee deserves your attention) but find ways to leverage your time. For example, work with them as a group. If there is no improvement, then use the "confronting problem performer" technique in Chapter 8.

Chapter 7
Commit to Consistent Coaching

Think about a great coach in your past. Do you have that special person in mind? What did he or she do that was so great?

I've heard many different answers to this question, including "she cared about my success," "he made me feel important," "she had high expectations of me," "he always listened to me," "she inspired me to get better," and "he was a great teacher."

What these answers all have in common is one thing: A rep's favorite coach was someone truly **committed** to their success. People don't remember a coach so much for the step-by-step coaching process that person used (though they probably had one). They remember coaches more for how those managers interacted and communicated and the effort they put into connecting with their team.

The analogy that always occurs to me when I explain the need for this commitment is an experience I had when I lived in a dry, hot California town for many years. My next-door neighbor had a good-sized front yard. During the summer, he would wait until the lawn was sickly looking and then put out his portable Rain Bird™ sprinkler and let it spew water for two hours. Clearly that water was either evaporating or running off because his lawn remained brown. My yard, by contrast, had a built-in sprinkler system that would pop up every day and water my lawn for maybe five minutes. I used less water than my neighbor but had a much greener lawn.

I think about coaching the same way. All too often we delay a coaching conversation until the sales rep produces a bad result. Then we plant what I've come to think of as a portable "rain bird of coaching" next to the rep, crank it on full blast, drench them in "advice" (likely interpreted as criticism), and expect them to flourish. I once had a client admit that his company does a lot of rain bird coaching. And he recognized that if you are a rain bird coach, it's like telling a rep, "If you're bad enough, I'll coach you!" Waiting until problems are severe then drowning your salesperson in a flood of feedback isn't helpful. That's not how people learn or improve.

This "rain bird of coaching" metaphor seems to help managers remember why they should provide more consistent coaching. But it raises another question in their minds: "How can I also be more consistent in my approach to coaching so the outcome is better results?" The answer to that question is using a model that reminds you of the sequential steps for having more meaningful and effective conversations with your reps. My version of such a model is called C.O.A.C.H., and it is the topic of the rest of this chapter.

The C.O.A.C.H. Model

C.O.A.C.H. stands for **C**ommit, **O**bserve, **A**ssess, **C**onsult, and **H**elp (Figure 18). I'll walk through each of these components next, but the key thing to notice is that the coaching conversation with a sales rep comes in the fourth step (Consult)—after you have gathered sufficient information to fully understand what the rep needs.

Figure 18: The C.O.A.C.H. Model

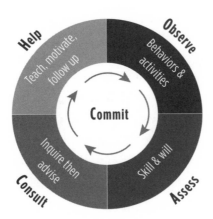

C.O.A.C.H. = Commit

I can tell that a sales manager is truly committed to helping their sales reps improve if their *behavior* is consistent with their *intent*. That is, they commit themselves to teaching reps to get better. They actively manage their time and priorities (as discussed in Chapter 2) so that they can spend more time on developmental coaching.

Every time you allow yourself to become distracted, to do a task that someone else can (and should) do, you prevent the accomplishment of something only you can do. Check your calendar for the past month and think about how you've spent your time. Did you devote sufficient time to developmental coaching so that all members of your team are better today than they were 30 days ago? If not, what do you need to do differently so your commitment to the development of your team is reflected in how you spend your time? I want you to commit to managing your calendar so you can coach every day. Not every other day. Not once a week. Every day. When you commit to teaching, and you follow through, every aspect of your coaching will improve.

The salesperson's commitment

A successful coaching relationship takes both a coach and a coach-ee. It does no good to spend your time on someone who isn't going to listen, learn, or change. A salesperson's commitment to the coaching process is tied to personality traits such as openness to feedback, acceptance of constructive criticism, interest in continued improvement, and motivation to succeed and constantly strive for new challenges and results—in brief, their coachability, which I addressed in Chapter 4.

C.**O**.A.C.H. = Observe

One of the sales instincts that sales managers have the hardest time overcoming is the urge to be a player (p.19) and instead embracing the role of an observer. As Yogi Berra once said, "You can observe a lot just by watching."

I once had a sales manager, for example, who noticed that I wasn't getting enough high-value appointments and then sat in on some prospecting calls to help me figure out why. In other words, he took the time to observe what I was doing (or, as it turned out, not doing)—which is a great example of the importance of early-cycle coaching. (See sidebar, p. 135.)

Yet too many sales managers go into a coaching conversation without spending enough time watching what a sales rep does. As a consequence, they can only offer superficial insights and general advice, neither of which is particularly helpful to a rep.

Early sales-cycle intervention

As it turned out, the mistake I was making occurred *in the first or second phone call with prospects.* And fortunately, I had a sales manager who didn't just get involved in big deals that were nearing a close. He paid attention to what his reps were doing through-out the full sales cycle. That way, he had a much big-ger impact on my success (and that of the rest of our team). Without that early intervention, I never would have solved my problem. I'll talk more about the importance of early-cycle sales coaching in Chapter 9.

The experience with my former manager shows why acting on your commitment to coaching has to start by observing your salespeople in action, such as in meetings with customers (either outside sales or inside sales) or in your sales team meetings. You can also "observe" the metrics of their work efforts in your CRM system.

While making any observation, you want to gather data in the form of notes on the following:

1. What people do

2. What they *don't* do

3. Their body language and/or tone of voice

When I was a sales manager, I found it helpful to have tools and checklists that would help me perform assessments like this and make sure I didn't miss anything important. You'll see an example of an observation checklist in Figure 19. The format I use guides me to look at three categories (general sales skills and wills, sales process skills, and preparation); you may have other categories in your own version. I would take this kind of form with me when I was doing a ride-along (or call-along) with a rep and enter my ratings as the day progressed.

Reminder: Observe, don't conclude!

One warning: There is a very natural human temptation to leap to conclusions when you observe someone. This is another instinct you have to fight as a sales manager.

When I work with sales managers, I ask them to give me some examples of observations they've made of a sales rep. What almost always happens is that they tell me about their *interpretations* of the rep's behavior—a conclusion they've reached about the rep's attitude (like Column 1 of Table I).

Jumping to conclusions will hinder your ability to provide effective coaching because you'll never know if your interpretations are right or wrong. And your reps will see you as judgmental and critical if you tackle them with interpretations instead of facts. In contrast, *observations* are clearer and more specific about an event, with no interpretation attached until you have a conversation with the rep about what is going on.

In observing your reps, you need to take notes on *what they actually do* (like the examples in Column 2 of Table I), not your interpretation of why they are doing it. You must be able to **describe specific behaviors** (or the lack of behaviors) to your sales reps. Do not use statements that could be considered judgmental. And be sure to catch the right as well as the wrong. (See sidebar, p. 138.)

Figure 19

Name: Manager: Date:

Rating Scale: 5-Very Strong   4-Strong   3-Good/Average
2-Needs Improvement   1-High-Priority Improvement

	Skill/Will Area	Rating	Comments
General skills & wills	Defines and achieves customer go-forward commitment		
	Engages customer		
	Presentation/demo skills		
	Identifies and contacts multiple decision makers		
	Listening skills		
	Makes changes based on previous feedback (coachability)		
Ability to move customer through their buying process	Identifies customer's current buying step		
	Identifies needs/problems		
	Identifies/shapes customer buying criteria		
	Matches customer needs and buying criteria to strengths of your products/services		
	Repackages weaknesses		
	Resolves customer concerns/objections		
	Negotiates and closes		
Preparation (work ethic)	Knowledge of customer/prospect business		
	Knowledge of your products/services		
	Knowledge of competition		
	Overall professionalism and organizational skills		

Comments/Action Plans:

Table I: Conclusions vs. Observations

1. Conclusion	2. Observation
Fred doesn't support the company.	Fred doesn't complete the weekly updates of our CRM tool.
Allison has a bad attitude.	Allison arrives late for meetings, doesn't contribute, and rolls her eyes frequently.

Catch the right, not just the wrong

One tip when observing your salespeople is to make sure you note things the person does right, not just what they do wrong. This is harder than it sounds! In their book *Managing Major Sales*,[25] Neil Rackham and Richard Ruff describe an experiment they conducted. They made a video of a sales call that was specially designed to have an even balance of both good and bad points. They then asked experienced sales managers to watch the video and pick out any points about selling that struck them as worthy of comment, either good or bad.

If the managers were unbiased, you would expect to see an approximate 50/50 split of good and bad behaviors as comments. But after the experiment, Rackham and Ruff found that 82 percent of the sales managers' comments were about bad points!

25 Neil Rackham and Richard Ruff, *Managing Major Sales: Practical Strategies for Improving Sales Effectiveness* (HarperBusiness, 1991).

Lesson: We sales managers focus a lot more on what's going wrong than on what's going right. Our proficiency at pointing out what's ineffective can play out in a coaching style that is perceived by salespeople as negative and condescending. So as Ken Blanchard, author of *The One Minute Manager*, says, "Catch them doing something right."

C.O.**A**.C.H. = Assess

Prescription without diagnosis is malpractice. This statement applies as much to sales coaching as it does to medicine. Assessing a coaching opportunity means thinking about the potential causes of what you observed and developing a preliminary solution. If you are unable to diagnose the reason for the sales performance problem, then the solution you offer to your sales rep won't work.

To help you perform this assessment, refer back to the Success Profile discussion in Chapter 3. Having a document that describes what skills and wills are characteristic of greatness will give you a clear picture in your mind of what behaviors and attitudes you want to see in a rep. You can then compare what you have observed with what you would like or expect to see in terms of sales results, activity, account development expectations, team member responsibilities, time management, sales skills, and attitudes.

As you make this comparison, think about what could be causing the problems you see and what actions may be required of the sales rep. (These are the topics you'll discuss with the rep in the next step, Consult.)

If you think the problem relates to a skill, the cause is usually a lack of experience or inadequate training or mentoring—either the person never learned the skills in the first place or was unable to translate classroom (or book) learning into action. The solution is to make sure your training programs are highly interactive and practical. Include one-on-one or small group teaching as needed, plus role-playing and perhaps mentoring to help the person learn the necessary tactics and steps.

If you think that poor will is at the root of the problem, consider that willingness problems often arise from one of two sources:

- **A lack of confidence.** One cause for a lack of confidence is unrealistic expectations. If a professional baseball player expected to get a base hit in every at bat, he would be disappointed most of the time. Though this expectation is unrealistic, the player could think they're failing if they don't bat 1.000. So if you run into a rep who seems discouraged, start by asking, "What is your expectation here?" If it is unrealistic, help the rep develop a more realistic understanding of what is possible given their stage of professional development. Going forward, be sure to praise their effort as well as results until their confidence has been restored. If their expectation is realistic, the underlying cause may actually be a skill issue (they aren't confident in their ability to be successful with a skill) or an experience issue (perhaps they tried and failed in the past). More training, mentoring, or role-playing might solve those kinds of confidence issues.

- **A lack of motivation.** You will see a lack of motivation either in a new or inexperienced rep who fails to improve or in an experienced rep who has "lost the fire" (that is, they were good producers in the past but no longer are). Such salespeople either never had or have lost sight of their personal goals. More specifically, the link between their behaviors and their personal goals/sales results is now broken. Because motivational issues are one of the most common and challenging coaching situations for managers, I've devoted the next chapter to this topic.

Focus, focus, focus

Most of us only have the capacity to improve one or two things at any given time. Learning—and especially skill development—occurs little by little over time, not all at once. What typically happens, however, is that a sales manager will give a sales rep a laundry list of things they need to improve. The rep feels overwhelmed, which undermines their self-confidence and is unlikely to result in meaningful change.

That's why my advice for dealing with these issues comes from two sources. First, there is my favorite golf pro. When I take a swing, he sees at least a half dozen flaws. But then he gives me just one suggestion, and that one suggestion solves many of my flaws. This is a great model for coaching, one that I advise for any sales manager.

Second is Andy Grove, former CEO of Intel. In his book *High Output Management*,[26] Grove advises us to write down both good and bad points about an employee and look for patterns among the items. You would, for example, make a complete list of a sales rep's strengths and developmental needs. Then you would look at the whole thing and try to **pick out the common thread** so you can ideally solve multiple problems with the same prescription. (See sidebar below.)

Finding a common thread

Suppose a sales rep's strength is a high amount of prospecting activity. Weaknesses include a low lead conversion rate and a low quote-to-close rate. What is a common link between those issues? Here's a hint: Think about high prospecting activity as a warning sign of the rep's inability to make appointments. When viewed that way, I can think of at least four possible

---

26 Andrew S. Grove, *High Output Management* (Vintage, 1995, 2nd ed.).

common threads between high prospecting and low conversions:

- The sales rep isn't asking second- or third-level diagnostic questions.
- The sales rep spends too much time talking about the exciting capabilities of your product/service, rather than focusing on underlying customer needs, problems, and solution requirements.
- The salesperson lacks the self-confidence to engage C-level prospects in a thought-provoking way.
- The salesperson lacks basic business acumen and is unable to connect with customers around their operational, strategic, or performance issues.

Once you have diagnosed the issue, look to the options I discussed for solutions: education or training to improve a skill, carefully constructed conversations to work on will, or role-playing to improve confidence.

Focusing on one or two areas that create multiple problems will have a higher payoff than trying to attack any single weakness alone. Coaching the symptoms of a problem instead of addressing the underlying causes can do more harm than good. So the next time you have a development discussion with a rep, think like my golf pro and Andy Grove. Pick out one or two of the most important things you want a salesperson to work on.

C.O.A.**C**.H. = Consult

Finally! The step where you get to share your wisdom with the sales rep. But not so fast. As you'll see, there are two substeps here: **inquire** then **advise**. It may sound odd to start off a Consult step by listening instead of talking, so let me explain.

Inquire

You've no doubt heard the catch phrase, "Telling is not selling." Well, *telling* is not *coaching* either. You have to engage people in their own development, which you can do by listening to their ideas first.

There are many ways to approach this inquiry. One is to paraphrase back to the salesperson what you heard them say and ask their opinion on how well it worked. For example, *what specific action did you want the prospect to take at the end of the meeting and was that agreed to? Why do you think that did [or did not] happen?*

Another alternative is to ask one or two general questions such as *what do you think went well? What are one or two things that you could improve on?*

Or, if you want the person to focus on a specific area, you can target your questions to that area:

- [Preparation] How did you prepare going into the meeting? Do you think you were prepared enough? What would you do differently the next time around?

- [Inquiry] How well do you think you did in asking questions of the customer?

- [Listening] How well did you listen to the prospect's answers? Do you think that the customer thought you were listening to them?

- [Structure] Did you keep and build interest?

- [Recovery after problems] Is there anything you could have done during the meeting to get it back on track?

- [Improvement] How and when can you get back in there, do it better, and get this opportunity moving again?

Starting off the Consult phase by asking questions does five things:

1. It engages the rep in the process of their own improvement.

2. It demonstrates your interest in hearing their thoughts and ideas.

3. It allows you to focus the rep's attention on skill or will issues you've identified as needing improvement.

4. It helps you evaluate their level of self-awareness.

5. It serves as a model of questioning that reps can use to coach themselves when you're not there. That speeds up their cycle of learning and helps them get better faster.

Listening is not just for Millennials

There's a lot of talk these days about how Millennials expect their workplaces to be highly participative. For example, they expect to be listened to and expect their ideas to be taken seriously.

I have no doubts this is true, but I think you'd do well to treat all sales reps with that level of respect.

Advise

After you've gotten the sales rep to think through some of the issues on their own by asking them directed questions, it's time to share your ideas and perspective with them. Tell them what you think they did well and one or two things you think they could improve (remember my golf pro and Andy Grove from the previous section). The "one thing" might be something like this:

- Doing a better job at developing the need

- Improving negotiation skills

- Understanding how to better position your offering(s) against the competition

- Being more enthusiastic about solving customer problems

- Supporting others on the team as they deal with changes

- Being willing to become a positive role model for the team

One more thing to keep in mind: When you deliver coaching in a more timely manner, the consequences of a salesperson's mistakes will often not yet be apparent. If the person made a mistake in the first few steps of selling, the impact may not be felt for weeks or months—not until the prospect balks at a price, haggles on details, or just stops communicating, for example. So it's important for you as the coach to make those connections clear. To wrap up the conversation, therefore, you need to **get buy-in on why a skill or strategy is important**. Challenge the rep to think through the consequences of what they have done or not done with an implied *why this is important* message buried in the question: *I noticed that you didn't ask about the prospect's decision criteria, but you went ahead and scheduled your demonstration for next week. How do you plan to organize your presentation to meet their needs?*

This discussion of why is especially important for Millennials (you may hear them ask "why should I do that?"). Their question is not a sign of resistance toward you; they just recognize that knowing the why helps them put their new learning in context.

C.O.A.C.H. = Help

Were you to stop the C.O.A.C.H. process after that second "C" (Consult), you would be leaving your reps to sink or swim on their own based solely on the insights you shared with them. That's a recipe for failure. To learn and change, your reps need and deserve whatever help you can offer them.

This lesson was brought home to me by the experience of an incredibly successful sales professional who was promoted into management. When Caroline became a manager, the idea of offering help to her sales reps didn't occur to her because she thought much of the job came naturally, as it had for her. If you asked her what made her successful, she couldn't explain it because she didn't have good self-awareness of what she was doing. She just didn't get why some of her reps struggled so much and wasn't curious enough to find out. As a result, she was quick to point out problems to her team but never offered them concrete help to improve. She was seen as a critic not a coach, and her reps were not improving. Needless to say, her team struggled to generate results.

What Caroline didn't realize is that when she became a sales manager, a crucial part of her job was teaching others how to do what she did.

When we make the transition from rep to manager, we have to be able to break down our skills into teachable chunks and explain them to our sales reps in a way that they can hear and learn the right lesson. Great sales managers know that everyone has strengths and weaknesses, that people learn in different ways, and that every salesperson needs customized help and support to get better. You and your salesperson need to agree on an action plan to improve the situation. You will need to raise the ideas you developed in the Assess phase (such as role-playing, training, goal setting, etc.), modified by any insights gained during the Consult conversation. Making these ideas a reality is what the Help step is all about. That help can come in one or more of the following three forms:

1. **Teaching**: Direct the rep to the appropriate training courses on a needed skill, or provide other instruction on how to perform a task or skill. Or demonstrate a skill, and then role-play with the student.

2. **Motivation**: If the problem is with wills and attitudes, the solution often has to include work to improve the rep's motivation, which requires in-depth one-on-one conversations. The next chapter provides different examples of how to coach willingness issues, but the basic points to discuss include why what you're requesting is important to you and your company, how to connect the desired change to their personal goals, and what will happen if the person fails to show improvement.

3. **Follow-up**: You've got to "inspect what you expect." Follow-up breeds accountability in your team. It sends the message that you want a sales rep to actually implement the results of your coaching conversation and make the changes that the two of you have agreed on. A sales manager who does not follow up sends a message to the salesperson that the coaching really wasn't all that important! So schedule specific follow-up sessions in your calendar (see sidebar, p. 148, for a tip). Be sure to check in with reps around intermediate milestones, not just for a desired final outcome. Provide regular feedback to the person by mentioning progress you've seen (or not seen) or asking them what they are struggling with.

A follow-up tip

How can you remember to follow up on every coaching conversation? Simple: Use the "Delay Sending Message" feature in Microsoft Outlook or a similar feature in the email system your business uses. Immediately after the coaching conversation, while it's fresh in your mind, compose an email to the sales rep following up on their commitment. Then select the "Delay Sending Message" feature in Outlook to schedule the next check-in point. Be sure to "cc" yourself as a reminder that you followed up!

Figure 20: Delay Sending Message

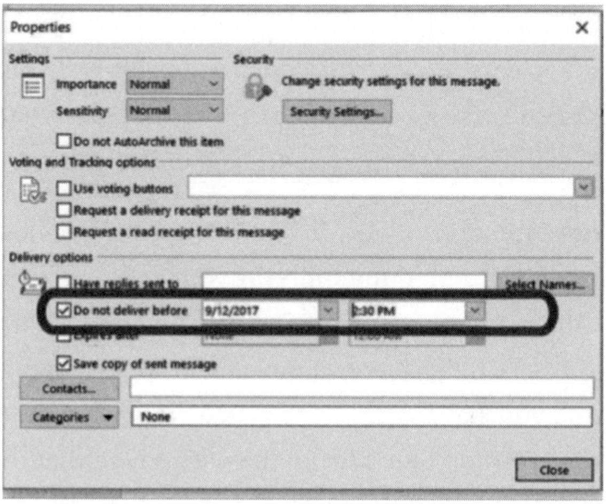

A Model of Consistent Coaching

One question I ask in all my seminars is "what is ineffective coaching?" People have no trouble coming up with examples. They talk about managers who wait too long before addressing a problem, those who do all the talking and no listening, and those who do not attempt to gain buy-in for needed changes.

And those answers are just the tip of the iceberg. There are sales coaches who focus on the wrong things because they haven't spent enough time diagnosing their team's skill or will deficiencies, or who don't know how to frame the issues in a way that illustrates the importance of doing a task a particular way (or not doing something the rep naturally does). Perhaps the rep doesn't act on the advice given, or the coach doesn't provide the right kind of follow up (to ensure the rep gets training, for example). And sometimes we sales managers forget the necessary components of a good coaching process.

While I've seen all of these problems in action, I was fortunate enough to have a sales manager early in my career who was the epitome of what to do right. I mentioned him earlier in this chapter concerning a mistake I was making in my initial contact with prospects. How that mistake got noticed and corrected is a good example of a consistent coach with a consistent approach.

At that time, I'd already established myself as a top sales producer. So when I sat down with my boss for a monthly one-on-one meeting, I had the smugness of a top dog. But he had reviewed my activity reports and commented that I just wasn't getting the same number of high-quality appointments that I'd gotten in the past. His plan, he said, was to sit in on some calls and provide me with specific feedback.

Today, as I look back on the mistakes I was making in my telephone approach—mistakes I was unaware of—I realize that I was likely suffering from "self-serving bias." A well-known principle in psychology, self-serving bias is the tendency for someone to see themselves as being more effective than they actually are. You see it when, for example, a sales rep who has a great month attributes their success to a strong work ethic and top-notch skills. But when that same rep has a bad month, they blame external factors, such as lousy leads from marketing. Sound familiar?

My manager was able to protect me from my self-serving bias in part because of what he *didn't* do. He didn't wait until my sales numbers started to fall off. He didn't just urge me to make more calls. He didn't tell me to try harder. He didn't step in and take over on my calls. He didn't wait until I thought a deal was nearing the close so he could ride in like a white knight and rescue the deal.

Above all, he didn't wait for me to *ask* for coaching. People with a self-serving bias don't ask for coaching, because they are unaware of the mistakes they are making. In my case, I would have kept losing deals I could have won, and kept blaming everything but my own approach for those losses.

You are the most talented sales professional on your team. However, your sales *management* success will ultimately be determined by how effective you are at instilling your greatness as a sales rep into the hearts and minds of your team members. The essence of coaching is helping your salespeople to learn what they don't already know—the skills and attitudes they need to maximize their success—and remind them of their skills when necessary. Because of the pervasive existence of the self-serving bias among sales teams, you are the *only* person who can accomplish this. Be a proactive sales coach. Take your coaching to your people.

Chapter 8

Motivate the Demotivated

During a webinar I recently delivered for about 150 sales managers, I asked them to indicate what percentage of performance problems on their team were mostly or largely due to problems with attitude or willingness. The options are listed below. What would you answer?

- 0%–24%

- 25%–49%

- 50%–74%

- 75%–100%

The most common answer was the third option (50%–74%) with the second option (25%–49%) almost as popular. Overall, the vast majority of participants thought a significant number of the performance issues they face on their team are due to bad attitudes—or what I call "willingness problems" (to contrast them with skill deficiencies).

This didn't surprise me. Deficiencies in will—a rep's attitude and mental approach to the job—are much more difficult to solve, and this is perhaps one reason why they get ignored so often.

Yet taking action is imperative. As I mentioned in Chapter 6, Robert Sutton cited a number of studies in his article in *The Wall Street Journal* a few years back that demonstrated having just one bad apple can bring a team's performance down by more than 30 percent, **no matter how good the rest of the group is**. (Even if a team is geographically remote, its members will get to know each other, and the negative impact will spread.) Many similar studies have found that poor behavior has a much stronger negative effect on a team than the positive effect of good behavior.

As Sutton writes in his WSJ article, "Having just a few nasty, lazy or incompetent characters around can ruin the performance of a team or an entire organization no matter how stellar the other employees." For a sales team, I'd add other descriptors for "bad apples," such as salespeople who are disrespectful of other team members (perhaps even the manager), unwilling to accept advice and sales coaching, satisfied with mediocre performance, or so focused on their own sales results that they don't mind trampling others to make their numbers. Remember that you hear and see only a small fraction of what your reps are saying and doing, so if you observe some negative behavior, it's always best to assume that the situation is worse than you are seeing.

Dealing with this wide range of willingness problems takes finesse. You can't send someone to a class to improve an attitude. You can't force someone to be more motivated simply by telling them what to do or cheerleading from the sidelines. As a sales director recently commented to me, "A will issue is a different conversation." And he's right.

Instead, you have to think about what will motivate—or what has demotivated—the person. (See sidebar, p. 153.) You have to talk to them in a way that prevents them from becoming defensive, or else the conversation will stop dead in its tracks. In this chapter, I'll give a brief refresher of some key motivation concepts, talk about the switch in mental attitude that *you* will need, and then give four examples of how these ideas play out in real life.

Don't confuse low confidence with low will

As I mentioned in Chapter 7, sometimes a lack of confidence (because of low skill) can be confused for a lack of will. If a salesperson has failed at a task in the past—such as making cold calls or delivering a presentation to a roomful of decision makers—they may anticipate that negative consequences will occur if they try it again.

If you observe that a sales rep fails to perform certain tasks or is very reluctant to do something, don't jump to the conclusion that they have a poor attitude. Probe first to see if they are simply lacking the confidence that they can do those tasks well. If yes, then the solution is to develop their skills (not adjust their attitude). You can use training, role-playing, mentoring, and coaching to address those skill issues.

Motivators and Demotivators

If you've done any research into motivation, you'll know that there are a lot of competing models. The one I find most helpful as a manager is shown in Figure 21. The graphic shows examples of both the positive factors, called **motivators**, that raise the natural level of motivation (providing incentives for people to improve and get better), and the negative factors, called **demotivators**, that rob people of their enthusiasm for the job.

Figure 21: Motivators vs. Demotivators

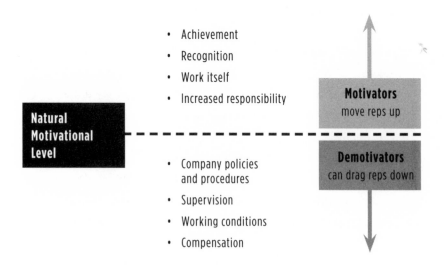

There are two things I always point out about this model:

- Motivators are intrinsic factors that address internal thoughts and emotions; demotivators are almost always extrinsic factors in the environment that people cannot control.

- There is no overlap between the two sets of factors. You cannot motivate people simply by removing demotivators and you cannot demotivate them simply by ignoring the motivators.

In sum, there is a big difference between being *un*motivated (not having enough motivators, which usually shows up as a lack of energy to engage) and being *de*motivated (being discouraged about the job).

As a sales manager you cannot control *what* will motivate or demotivate people—both demotivators and motivators are deeply personal. That means you'll have do some digging to figure out what will provide an incentive for each person to not only do a good job but also maintain their energy and desire to keep improving on the job. You'll also have to figure out if there are issues in the workplace that they find demotivating.

Truth be told, dealing with demotivators is difficult. Review the list of four typical demotivators in Figure 21, and it's evident that neither you nor the rep has much control over those factors (except supervision). But if you know what is demotivating them, you can try to find ways to limit the impact of those factors and shift the rep's attention toward positive motivators.

Luckily, dealing with the unmotivated is easier because there are motivators that you do have a lot of control over. The four listed in Figure 21—achievement, recognition, work itself, and increased responsibility—show up in many models these days, but they all trace back to the work of Frederick Herzberg, the famed motivation specialist whose research began in the 1950s.[27] Here's how I translate his ideas into the sales environment.

- **Achievement:** The perception the sales rep has that they are improving. This factor is one reason why the Success Profile is such an important tool—reviewing it regularly helps salespeople clearly see that they are getting better. In addition to using the Success Profile, give the rep specific comments about the skills and abilities they have improved ("this is perhaps the best presentation you've delivered because _____").

- **Recognition:** It never ceases to amaze me what some salespeople will do for a plaque! So while some companies go overboard in terms of recognition, you don't have to follow that

---

27 See *The Motivation to Work*, originally published in 1959, then re-released several times since then. Currently available in the paperback version with co-authors Bernard Mausner and Barbara Bloch Snyderman (Transaction Publishers, 1993).

model. Many forms of recognition don't cost much if anything. You can, for example, bring a salesperson to a senior leadership meeting, create a contest, celebrate their successes at a team meeting, and so on.

- **Work itself:** The best sales reps I've ever worked with are people who enjoyed the job of selling. Part of their reward was simply doing a good job. To use this factor as a motivator, you'll need to find ways to add more meaning to the job. One way is to link a rep's work to a larger goal or purpose. Help them understand *why* their work matters. Be assured that people will find value in knowing how their work contributes to the goals of your company and the greater good of serving your customers.

- **Increased responsibility:** Some people are motivated by the desire to expand their job duties and perhaps even move up the food chain. (Adding more responsibilities to a rep's job is actually a form of recognition that the manager has confidence in a rep's abilities and trusts them to do a job well.) There are many simple ways to do this. Involve reps in some of the decisions that you have to make. Or assign them to do a ride-along with a job candidate you are considering hiring, and then ask them to share their thoughts and analysis afterward as an acknowledgment that you value their opinion. Or ask reps who have demonstrated their competence to take the lead on important projects.

As I mentioned earlier, you cannot control which of these factors will motivate a rep, but you *can* control how much time you spend investigating the motivators for your team members. You just have to take the time to figure out which are most important to each rep and incorporate those factors into your discussions with the rep and into their personal development plans.

Money as a motivator

You may have noticed that money is not included in Frederick Herzberg's list of motivators. Numerous studies have revealed that, in general, money is not as big a motivator as most of us have been led to believe. Yet when you ask salespeople what motivates them, that's often their first answer. Since it's often money-oriented people who are attracted to the profession because of the earning potential, I think that money is more important in sales than in other jobs. But the degree to which money motivates people varies a lot. Plus, for most people it's not the money per se but what they want to do with the money that is the true motivator.

Here's how I address money: If a rep indicates they are motivated by money, I have them link their desired income to something they want to achieve, if they haven't already done so. This is what I call the *money goal*. Ask them: *If you could meet your income goal, what would you do with the extra income?*

If they can't answer with something concrete right away, tell them to think about it and come back to you. A vague goal of "more money" doesn't provide as much motivation as "I want to take a trip to Europe" or "I want to buy a new car" or "My kid starts college next year."

I once had a sales rep, for example, who told me he wanted to sell $250,000 more in product in the coming year. That was ambitious! I asked him, "What will you do with the extra money you'll make when you achieve your goal?" The rep couldn't answer right away. But he came back the next day and said, "I want to buy a BMW 3-Series."

So I went down to the local BMW dealer and brought back a brochure on the specific car he wanted. The sales rep cut a picture out of the brochure and taped it to his bathroom mirror so he would see it every morning as he was preparing to go to work. He made the stretch goal quite easily and bought the car.

Lessons from the Wrong End of Poor Coaching

I remember it like it was yesterday. My area VP called and said that he planned to stop by my office in a few days to talk about something important. Because I'd recently been named "GM of the Year: West Region," I assumed that he wanted to discuss a possible promotion.

He arrived at my office, sat down, and said, "Kevin, I'm here because recently I've become really concerned about your lack of commitment to this company."

I was stunned. How did I go from the hero to a slouch in just two months? How could he possibly think I lacked commitment?

My boss continued, sharing his reasons for his observation about my lack of commitment, but I wasn't listening. He had just said something that I personally disagreed with. I thought he was full of it and so I shut down.

My boss's judgmental comment was jarring since at that time I was confident that I deserved that "GM of the Year" award. His comments came across as a personal attack and my immediate response was defensiveness. His approach also depleted some of my commitment—which means that in this conversation he achieved the exact opposite of what he wanted! (Some time after this conversation, I realized that a change in my job description and the company's compensation plan resulted in me seeming to be less committed to the organization, even though I wasn't conscious of it. But this after-the-fact realization was too late to change the nature or impact of this initial conversation with my boss.)

Dealing with demotivation issues is very challenging for sales managers. The big picture you want to keep in mind is how to confront the situation in a way that results in increasing your rep's level of motivation. How do you *not* make the problem worse?

Being on the wrong end of a "poor will" discussion, and my own experiences dealing with demotivated reps, taught me that sales managers dealing with willingness issues have to do three things:

- **Put their dominant self in "park."** People with bad attitudes, in most cases, don't recognize it in themselves. I sure didn't. If you take a direct approach with a demotivated rep, it will come as a surprise, and they will likely become defensive (as I did). If you are blunt, people will resist. They may speak their objections or, like me, simply sit silent and detached.

- **Probe for the source of unwillingness before prescribing a solution.** You have no idea, really, what the source of the poor attitude is. Perhaps the rep is unhappy with a recent change in the organization—compensation plans, territory alignment, organizational structure, job responsibilities, and so on. Or perhaps there is something in their personal life (relationship issues, illness, etc.) that is robbing them of energy and enthusiasm. Or it could be a combination of these factors.

- **Comment on specific behavioral observations rather than jump to conclusions.** You have to separate the unacceptable behavior from the person. If you sound judgmental of them as a person, you will never make progress.

Using these tactics, you can approach reps in a non-accusatory way and communicate your expectations that they will now conform to the high standards you've set for your team. Let me explore this theme a little more.

Becoming a helper instead of a critic

Your instincts tell you to be direct and to the point. But if you start off telling the rep they aren't motivated or have lost their commitment or fire or have a lousy attitude, they will resist. And the trust bond that you have worked so hard to establish could be damaged or perhaps ruined.

What do you do instead? **Switch your mindset to help mode.** Be curious and ask a series of diagnostic questions. These are your goals for the conversation:

- Create receptivity at the beginning of the conversation.

- Figure out what *they* are thinking and why (not telling them what you are thinking).

- Have both of you agree on whether the rep has a performance or attitude problem and exactly what that problem is.

- Identify the contributors to the problem. What has changed recently that led them to where they are now?

- Make sure, by the end of the discussion, that the rep understands the consequences if a change isn't made.

Here are four examples of how to weave the ideas of motivators, demotivators, and help mode together to structure one-on-one conversations with reps who have poor will.

A comment on the well-known sandwich technique

Many sales managers have been taught to use what's called a sandwich technique to communicate their dissatisfaction with a rep's behavior. In this technique, a negative (or "constructive") comment is slipped between two positives. It's an attempt by the manager to soften the blow.

Personally, I'm not a fan of this technique because you end up sending mixed messages, which is confusing to the rep. Should they be pleased or concerned? Plus, in practice the salesperson often misses the central message that they need to change something in their behavior and instead chooses to focus on the positive things the manager said.

Scenario 1: Re-energizing a Good Rep Gone Stale

Do you have a rep who was a good producer in the past but whose results have fallen flat—or even gotten worse?

Start off a conversation with this kind of rep with something like this: "There's something going on with your performance that I don't really understand. I was hoping we could talk about it."

Then ask a very open-ended question: "What's been happening with you lately?" Listen to their answer and then steer the conversation accordingly.

If the person does not acknowledge the problem, then you have to get them to recognize that something has changed. Ask them how they would evaluate their own performance and how they think they're doing now compared to six months ago. Find out what metrics they pay attention to. Provide productivity numbers and observations of specific changes you have seen in their behavior. Be factual, not judgmental.

If the person admits that they have simply been complacent, your goal is to help re-ignite the fire. Find out what will motivate them—more money or more responsibility, for example. Revisit the rep's personal goals: "What's your number one professional goal over the next twelve months?" Discuss specific actions they can take to meet those goals.

If there is something personal happening, discuss ways that you can accommodate their needs without jeopardizing the team's morale or performance. As I mentioned earlier, one bad apple really can ruin the whole bunch!

Scenario 2: Dealing with the "Uncoachable" Prima Donna

Recently, I was working with a team of sales managers and this question came up: "How do I handle a salesperson who sells a lot but is uncoachable?" I call good producers with poor attitudes **prima donnas** (also known as **"troubled talent"**); they generally get good numbers, but they don't seem to care about anyone else on the team, including their manager. It's a common issue.

I had a prima donna on the team I discussed in Chapter 6, for example. She is portrayed by Carlotta Tendant in the ratings table that I referenced in that chapter (reprinted here in Table J).

Table J: Differences in Top Performers

Name	Skill	Will
Ann T. Oxidant	5	5
Clare Voyant	2	3
Sal Monella	3	5
Willy Sellmore	2	2
Carlotta Tendant	5	2
Al Fresco	4	4

Unfortunately for me and our team, Carlotta had a very poor attitude and very little will to improve or contribute to the team. She was responsive to external customers but extremely negative and condescending to her internal customers. At some point in her career, Carlotta's sales manager (someone before my time) failed to address her poor attitude. And she thought, *hey, you haven't said anything. You haven't confronted me. So it must be OK.* She put herself above the team.

In some ways, passionate, hardworking, experienced, and talented people deserve to be treated differently. They consider this special treatment a form of recognition. But in other ways—determined by you—they must be treated exactly the same as everybody else. You must actively manage this situation, and manage *everyone* on your team to your expectations around behavior and attitude as well as results. (See the comment in Chapter 6 on p. 124 about consistently enforcing standards.)

Before they talk with a prima donna, I challenge sales managers to first look in a mirror. I want them to acknowledge that maybe they are part of the problem. Admit it. We sales managers rarely try to manage *attitudes*, especially if a salesperson is making their numbers. We look the other way, ignoring the negative impact on the team. We make exceptions, which serves to reinforce the prima donna's notion that they are special. What you don't confront you condone. So if you've let poor attitudes go by unremarked in the past, you have to own up to that fact and indicate that you are making a change going forward.

Prima donnas generally don't know or don't care about their impact on the team. They will resist if you simply try to tell them to behave differently, but you can **use their ignorance of their own negative behavior to your advantage**. (The hidden agenda here is to increase the troubled talent's awareness of the specific *positive* behaviors they need and do it in such a way that you don't tick them off!)

The strategy I use starts by trying to increase the person's sense of *team* responsibilities:

1. Make a list of the top five attitudinal qualities that characterize—in your eyes—a salesperson with a great attitude (refer to your Success Profile, if you have one).

2. Share the list with the prima donna. Sit down with the person one-on-one. Show them the list and explain why it's important to you that the entire team adopts these behaviors.

3. Ask the prima donna for their ideas. Do they agree with your list? Do they think these things are important for team success? What would they add or change on the list? (This demonstrates you respect their opinion.)

4. Appeal to their vanity by asking them to step up as a team leader and help you roll out the new standards. Tell them that their support is crucial for team buy-in.

5. Hold a full team meeting where you share the list of positive attributes with the entire sales team. Share the spotlight with

the prima donna, perhaps having the rep share stories from their experience that relate to the positive attributes.

Ideally, this will reengage the prima donna in caring about the team's success, not just their own. No matter what, however, you have to be clear about your expectations for them going forward. If this doesn't work, you may need to escalate (see Scenario 4: Confronting Continuing Problems later in this chapter).

Scenario 3: Encouraging a Disillusioned Beginner

This rep, in the not too distant past, was an enthusiastic newbie, a rep who came in as a new hire, applied your system, and had some big early wins. But they made a crucial mistake—they followed opportunities through the funnel but forgot to continue to work "above the funnel" (do the spadework needed to get more new opportunities into the pipeline). So they're on a sales rollercoaster that's currently headed downward.

This kind of cycle is very common with new reps. Your challenge is to help them maintain their enthusiasm while pushing through this mentally challenging period. By providing both direction and support, you can ensure they ride back up sooner rather than later.

So again, you're not going to just tell them what to do. You're going to sit down and talk to them about ways you can help them emerge victorious from what is sure to be a temporary downturn.

Inspire them by offering encouragement and examples of other salespeople who went through a similar rough patch. Ask them what they think they need the most help with to improve and offer your own tips. Then make plans accordingly (more training? mentoring? coaching?). What can they do to develop solid work habits that will help them build a strong territory and prevent the situation from recurring? Get them to see the bigger picture—and the pride they will feel if they allow themselves a little more time to grow and improve.

Scenario 4: Confronting Continuing Problems

Have you ever been frustrated by a thickheaded sales rep whom you've coached over and over and over again but they don't get the message? Or by a rep who simply refuses to acknowledge that their behavior is a problem? So have I!

What can you do when all else has failed? There's one last step I recommend before de-hiring someone, which I call the **Problem-Cause-Solution-Two Roads** or **PCST** method. (I usually pronounce PCST like a word instead of spelling out the letters; the result is a sound that exemplifies the despair we managers often feel at this stage of dealing with a recalcitrant rep.)

I have to acknowledge that the main purpose here is not so much to understand what's going on with the rep—which, I would hope, was your attitude prior to this point—but to escort them to the intersection of choice and help them clearly see the consequences if they do not change. I view PCST as my last, best hope for rectifying the problem and saving the rep.

Problem-CST

When talking with the sales rep, you need to be very clear about what the problem is and prepared to describe what the person *is* or *is not* doing that is creating the problem. By this point in your relationship with the person, you should have plenty of fodder: evidence from behaviors you have observed and prior conversations and agreements. For example, are they failing to follow through on certain commitments? Are they not being persistent enough with prospects? Are they continuing to say sarcastic things about your company in meetings?

The goal of this part of the conversation is to reach an agreement with the salesperson about what the problem is and the impact it is having on both the rep and the team. You could start off with this question:

Is your current level of performance acceptable to you?

If they answer "yes," then you need to probe into why they think that and steer them in a direction to consider the factors that you are considering:

How are you evaluating your performance?

What about _____? (Name a will that you've noticed they are poor in.) How would you rate yourself in that area? What do you think the impact is on you and the team?

If they reply "no" (meaning they are not happy with their performance), then both of you can agree that the rep's performance is not up to expectations. If you want, you can probe for details ("What are you unhappy with in your performance?") or you can move on to the next step, looking for causes.

P-Cause-ST

If you don't know the *why* of someone's behavior, it's difficult to develop solutions that will help the person change. (See the "prescription without diagnosis is malpractice" discussion on p. 139.) Your ability to help your rep see the underlying reasons for what they've been doing or not doing is crucial for coaching success. If the rep doesn't acknowledge the potential causes, any solutions will be wasted.

You will likely need to dig a little to uncover the root causes that are contributing to the rep's poor will. Since you've just agreed on the description of the problem (right?), and both of you know that the problem is long-standing (otherwise you both wouldn't be in this situation), you have to get the rep to think a little deeper. Here's some wording to get you started:

> *We've been dealing with this problem for a while. What do you think is going on? Why do you think you haven't followed through on our previous discussion?*

> *What barriers have been preventing you from making the change and achieving the goals we've discussed?*

PC-Solution-T

Once you and the rep have agreed on the problem, its impact, and its causes, the time has come to talk about what the solution should look like. You need to have an improvement plan in mind *before* you talk to the salesperson so you can be specific about what steps the rep needs to take and by when. You may need to modify it slightly on the fly to accommodate any new insights gained in the previous two steps, but the purpose of Problem and Cause were really to get *the rep* to appreciate the nature and extent of the issue. Now, it's time for you to describe the following:

- What you want to see happen—the behaviors, activities, and results that you need to see going forward

- How you will monitor the rep to see if the changes are made

- What kind of timeline you will allow the rep (a week? two weeks? a month?)

When you're sure the rep is clear about these elements, move into the Two Roads section.

PCS-Two Roads

The last step of the PCST model is the most critical. You have to make it clear to the rep that they have reached a fork in the road and that going forward there are only two options open to them, one with negative consequences and one with positive consequences.

If they take the solution path that you've just discussed with them, then positive things will happen—and you should be able to describe for them what those positive things are.

If the person continues down the path they're on now, however—meaning they don't make the changes you are requesting—there will be negative consequences. Those could include everything from a loss of certain privileges to actually letting the salesperson go. (While obviously you would never terminate an employee as the first step in dealing with a problem, at this point, that may be a real possibility you need to come to grips with yourself before you have this conversation.)

Finally, the day after the conversation, follow up with the rep and ask if they have any questions about what you discussed and if they have feedback for you. Ask them to clearly define for you the choices they face, as a way to check that they heard and remember what you told them.

No matter what, remember that you can't control the outcome of this conversation. It's the rep's problem and their choice of which road they want to take. But you will have succeeded if the rep clearly understands the choice in front of them.

PCST in practice

I recently talked with a sales manager about a problem he had with a sales rep he considered a good performer but who wasn't complying with a company mandate to update the CRM tool daily. The salesperson's explanation was that she was too busy selling, plus her new accounts were having a lot of problems with installation and she had to spend time chasing down problems that weren't her fault. And then she said to the manager, "Would you rather have me spend my time selling and helping customers or putting data into a computer?"

Good question, right? The answer, of course, is that to be successful in this company, she needed to do both. But to combat her resistance to change, the sales manager had to be well prepared.

I asked him to think through the PCST components in preparation for a third conversation with this rep, and he got off to a great start. Here is a simplified version of his analysis:

- **Problem:** Sales rep not updating CRM tool daily.

- **Cause:** Lack of discipline or commitment to company requirement.

- **Solution to propose:** Rep hardwires 15 minutes into her schedule at the end of each day to do CRM updating.

Notice something missing? The sales manager described what he wanted to cover in the upcoming difficult conversation with this sales rep, but hadn't included the Two Roads element. I wasn't too surprised. Ignoring or mishandling the Two Roads part of a discussion with a problem performer, especially one who sells a lot, is a common issue for many sales managers.

So I said to the manager, "Exactly what are going to be the consequences for this rep if she does not change? If there are no consequences, her behavior will not change. Something good *has* to happen if she changes, and something *bad* has to happen if she doesn't change. If you don't have the answers, don't bother having this conversation."

If a rep's problem is poor sales performance, the options are very clear—they need to sell more or they will be off the sales team.

But often, as with the woman who wasn't using the company's CRM tool, the rep's performance isn't so bad that you'd want to fire them. This particular rep had proven herself to be a good producer. So what other options does a manager in this situation have?

To answer that question, the manager needs to know what is motivating the salesperson. Is it money? Opportunity? Responsibility? Are there privileges, perks, or sales lead rotation that the rep has now that could be taken away?

As it turned out in this case, this rep had expressed an interest in moving up into sales management in the future. So the Two Roads part of the discussion went something like this:

"Using CRM is a critical component in our company's strategy. If you continue to ignore your responsibility to use CRM, you will never be considered for a sales management position. Since my many conversations with you about this matter have not been successful, if yet another conversation becomes necessary, I'll need to ask my boss to join our conversation. And I really don't want to do that.

"If you change, however, and find just 15 minutes *every day* for CRM updates, then senior leadership will come to know you as someone who can be counted on to support and implement the company's priorities, and your name will still be in the running when a sales management opening occurs."

Tips for using PCST

Getting good at using the PCST approach takes some practice. Here are some tips:

Timely—Act as soon as you notice that the rep has failed to address a problem you've previously talked about with them.

Well planned—Think through what you want to say for each part of the PCST discussion. You've discussed the issue with the person before, so you should be able to anticipate their responses to some extent.

Behavior-oriented—Don't criticize the person. (Some salespeople are hypersensitive to criticism. Your goal is behavior change.) Talk about the behavior you need to see going forward.

Focused—Salespeople do have the gift of gab and many will use their verbal skills to sidestep uncomfortable situations. So make sure you don't allow the conversation to be diverted. Stick to your talking points. If the person attempts to divert the conversation, bring them back to the behavior.

Implementable—You need to provide the rep with a fair way to measure their own progress and to tell whether they have made the change you are requesting.

Future-focused—The rep cannot change the past, they can only change the future. So don't rehash grounds you've gone over multiple times already. Keep the discussion focused on what needs to change going forward.

Put the shoe on their foot—Consider saying to them, "Put yourself in my shoes. Suppose you had a rep who was doing what you're doing. What would you do?"

Your Own Moment of Truth

There is an element of playacting in sales management. And dealing with poor will and attitude calls for you to adopt a counterintuitive approach. You cannot be as direct as you might like, even if you tell yourself that you are dealing with the problem in a way that is in the best interests of the rep.

As the saying goes, people don't quit companies—they quit managers. Simply put: If you don't handle these discussions well, it could and likely will reflect poorly on your skills as a sales manager. So do what great sales coaches do. Stop and think: *How can I have the greatest possible positive influence on this rep and the situation?* These are the moments of truth that will define how effective or ineffective you are as a sales team leader.

Chapter 9
Increase Win Rates with Buying-Cycle Coaching

A sales VP who attended one of my workshops told me her main aha moment came when I challenged the audience to think about how they really know what the customer is doing at each step of the sales process since the customer's actions are a much better indicator of progress than a sales rep's actions.

As she thought about her own company's sales funnel, the sales VP realized that it didn't reflect customer actions at all. And the "won-lost" analysis her sales organization did occurred far too late in the sales cycle. That created a disconnect that made it hard to identify the mistakes that led to a loss—and obviously did no good in helping a sales rep repair the damage and salvage an endangered deal.

The sales VP told me, "Before now, if a salesperson told us that they'd nailed a presentation or had a sale that was a sure-thing, we'd believe them. But now I realize we have to get some validation based on what our customers are doing. That means we have to adopt a more investigative coaching style and get involved much earlier in the sales process."

Her company began by doing the work I described in Chapter 5: redefining the sales process and CRM to have a buying focus and defining exit criteria based on customer buying behavior. She then made sure her sales managers shifted their coaching questions so that reps would start to think more about this perspective as well. And results improved.

As this sales VP's company demonstrates, it's not just the sales funnels and CRM systems that benefit from having a customer focus. Sales coaching has to be shifted in that direction as well. What that means—and the impact it has—is the subject of this chapter.

Creating a Buying Perspective

When a company adopts a buying-process focus, part of a sales manager's responsibility becomes reinforcing that perspective in their dealings with sales reps. They must make sure that reps do the following:

- **See the process through the customer's eyes.** Rather than focusing on the steps of the sales process, which is usually all they've been taught up to now, sales reps must learn to appreciate the steps a customer goes through when making a buying decision.

- **Resist the urge to "prematurely pitch."** Talking about features and benefits of a solution does no good if the customer has not even decided to buy yet. Pitching benefits too soon is one main way that reps get out of sync with customer buying. Sales managers must encourage reps to make sure that a customer is prepared to appreciate the solution's benefits before the rep talks about them.

- **Focus on questions that get at the customer's go-forward actions (exit criteria).** Sales managers can demonstrate how to plan a sales call simply by asking reps the questions those reps should be asking themselves, such as "Where is this prospect at in their decision-making process?" and "What does this customer need to learn in order to take their next buying step?" and "What action do I want the customer to take after this call (or meeting)?"

The sales VP whose company I referenced at the beginning of this chapter has implemented this approach using the buying model I developed. It was introduced in Chapter 5, and I'll repeat it here for easy reference (Figure 22). Again you can use any model you like as long as the steps reflect what your customers do, not what your reps do!

Figure 22: Buying Steps

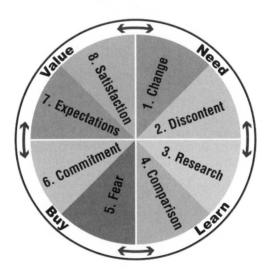

Here are some sample questions that the sales VP's managers ask their reps based on the buying process they identified:

- When a prospect is in the Change or Discontent step, a sales manager will talk to the rep about how many decision makers the rep has reached, what is important to those decision makers, and what buying criteria will play a big role in their decision.

The manager will ask the rep, "What is the title of the decision maker you've been meeting with? What do they care about most? What other decision makers are you trying to reach or would you like to reach?" (As an aside, reps document this information in the CRM system, which allows the sales VP and her managers to compare records from different sales and see what level of decision makers the reps have been meeting with on opportunities both large and small.)

- When a prospect is in the Comparison step—in which they compare alternative solutions available in the marketplace and decide which vendor they prefer—sales managers ask the rep, "Who is our competition? What will the customer think are our strongest points compared to that competition? Where are we weak?" A sales rep who is clueless about who they are up against is not prepared to deliver a presentation or write a proposal.

- When a prospect enters the Fear stage—the buying step that accounts for the natural hesitancy most customers feel when facing a major decision—the sales managers help guide reps in dealing with "sure thing" buyers who may have turned skittish. They will ask reps questions such as "What is your strategy for maintaining communication with the prospect after your demo? How are you going to follow up if the prospect doesn't respond right away? Have they expressed any concerns that you think might be causing them to pause now? What could you do to further address those issues?"

The sales VP told me that having coaches ask buying-focused questions of reps serves two purposes: First, as I promised to her, it helps them get greater insights into what is happening inside their customers and therefore ensures more realistic forecasts. Second, and equally important, it helps managers understand at a much deeper level where their reps are strong and where they are weak. Managers can then more easily get a rep to focus on the specific things they need to do to move a customer forward through the buying process. That means reps are having greater success.

Early-Cycle Sales Coaching

A beneficial consequence of having a customer focus is that sales managers end up getting involved with opportunities much earlier than ever before. The necessity of doing so is illustrated by the experience of another company I worked with. I recently caught up with the director of sales for this company. He'd come to me for help some months ago. He had told me that his company sells a high-tech product whose benefits aren't easy to explain. "We've already sold to all the companies that are early adopters, the ones who already knew they needed a product like ours. Now we're having a much harder time closing deals. Our old approach to selling just isn't working any more. What can I do to help improve our closing ratio?"

I asked if he had any thoughts about what the problem was.

"First off, our customers don't know that they have problems we can solve," he said. "My salespeople are very good at describing the benefits of our product, but it just doesn't connect with prospects.

"Another problem is that our competitors have been better than us at seeding the market with messages," he added. "Our prospects keep parroting back our competitors' language to us. So prospects are framing the issues in ways that make it harder for us to sell *our* unique strengths."

I asked what he had done so far, and he talked about holding more pre-close meetings with sales reps to review all of the steps and make sure the rep had done everything required up to that point. But it hadn't done any good.

I told this director that his approach was typical but had a fatal flaw. "You can't improve closing ratios by going in at the *end* of the sales process," I said. "You have to fix what your salespeople are doing at the very *beginning*—what they are doing to understand the customer's buying process. Those first few meetings are when a customer decides whether they have a problem that you can fix and whether it's worth their time to fix it. It's also where, from the customer's perspective, the size of the sale is determined. If you don't get your salespeople to probe those issues, no amount of finesse at the end stages is going to secure a deal for you."

Slowing down to sell faster

With my help, this sales director worked for about six months to implement all of the things I just talked about here and in earlier chapters (becoming more buying-focused in their sales model, sales training, CRM Sales Playbook, and coaching). When he called me again to reconnect, he wanted to update me on the results they'd seen.

"Our closing ratio has gone up across all our offices. Every office has taken a leap in their ability to close sales faster," he said.

I asked him what had made the difference.

He told me the focus on getting reps to better understand the customer very early on was the biggest factor. "We have found that having reps slow down to take more time in the first discussions with prospects has improved our ability to close more deals quicker," he said.

He then mentioned two specific things his sales force was doing now because of the different way their managers were coaching them:

1. In either the initial contact or the very first meeting, they spend a lot more time asking questions that get the customer to think about the problems they have. "Instead of us talking about benefits, the customer is recognizing for themselves that they have a need that we can fix," he said.

2. His salespeople all know how to "get the numbers," as he put it: helping the customer think through issues like what

the problem is costing them, the percentage of their business affected by the problems, and the number of jobs lost to inefficiency or the number that could be added if the customer's company could improve in this key area.

With this information, the director said, his salespeople are much better at "bringing the customer to the concept" much faster than ever before. "It's the prospect who sees the need for a product like ours," he explained. "They also have a better appreciation of all the costs they can incur if they do nothing. Once the benefits of action and consequences of inaction are clearer, they're much more motivated to buy."

His final comment to me was, "I've seen some of the best salespeople in our company fail because they were just trying to be salespeople. They were only thinking about their sales steps. They didn't understand the process from the buyer's seat—why that particular prospect may be looking to buy. Now that my sales force has that new perspective—and my sales managers are continually reinforcing that focus—my reps are much more effective."

"Slow down" really means "don't rush"

Since 2011 when my book *Slow Down, Sell Faster!* came out, the phrase "slow down" has been one of my favorite mantras for salespeople. I can't help but notice how often it pops up in other contexts. In February 2015, for example, NBA star Jason Kidd wrote an article called "The Best Basketball Advice I Ever Got."[28] Kidd's most important lesson ever? "Slow down," or as he says it, "Slowwww dowwwn."

28 http://www.theplayerstribune.com/jason-kidd-basketball-advice

Coming into the NBA, Kidd knew that speed was one of his assets. So naturally the advice to slow down didn't connect with him. In this article, he reflects on his career, and says he realizes his mistake was having only one gear: fast. He needed to be able to slow down.

When Kidd slowed down, his number of options on what to do with the basketball increased. Passing lanes opened up. Kidd writes, "You can't force spacing or timing—you gotta let it develop."

Now that he's a coach, Kidd sees young players making the same mistake he did. His job? Getting them to understand that "slowing down doesn't mean taking it easy. It's about not rushing."

Changing the Coaching Conversations

As you can see, developing a customer-buying focus changes the nature of coaching conversations dramatically. To help sales managers make this transition, I advise companies to develop a "coaching guide" built around the exit criteria that capture key customer actions you will see if they are moving forward in their buying process. As I discussed in Chapter 5, exit criteria are the specific actions that customers take that signal they are moving from one stage of buying to the next. By focusing your coaching on exit criteria, you are getting reps to think more about buying from the customer's perspective.

You can see an excerpt of the coaching guide that I helped the sales VP and his company develop in Figure 23. For each step of the customer's buying process, the company identified the exit criteria. They then went one step further and identified what questions the sales manager could ask of a rep to see if the rep was prepared to deal with a customer in that stage of buying.

Figure 23: Excerpt from a Coaching Guide

Buying Steps	Exit Criteria	Coaching Questions
Change	Interest confirmed by influential key stakeholder; agreement to first meeting	• With whom will you have the first meeting? • What problem is this person interested in solving?
Discontent (Acknowledge something needs to change)	Problems and causes of problems understood; economic implications and costs defined; "solution vision" stated; access to funds assured; stakeholders aligned	• What are this prospect's problems? What are the causes (in the customer's voice)? • What are the consequences of this problem(s) and their costs? • What is the impact if the customer decides to delay? • Who will make the funds available?
Research (Buying criteria defined)	Intangible criteria defined in tangible terms; proposals required	• Have you identified at least seven buying criteria for each decision maker? • Which of these criteria represent a threat to us? How will you handle that? • Which criteria can you connect to our company strengths? How will you do this?

You as a manager can use these coaching questions with a rep either before a conversation with a prospect or customer (pre-call planning) or afterward as a way to detect and diagnose any potential problems (post-call debrief). Either way, these coaching questions get the rep to think more deeply about a customer's buying process and what they can do to have the best shot at moving the opportunity down the funnel. Let's look at a few examples.

Less defensiveness with a customer-buying focus

Sales managers who have switched to a buying-centered approach tell me that it has made coaching sessions with all reps—both novice and experienced—much easier. Why? Because the conversations are focused on what *process steps* the rep has followed (or anticipates using) and what is needed to move a customer forward. That creates a much different tone than "what went wrong with this deal from last month," which tends to make reps defensive.

1. Pre-call planning

To get sales reps into the right mindset, sales managers should challenge them to think about their customer's buying behavior. Here are three standard questions I tell sales managers to ask:

1. **Where is the customer in their buying process?** This question gets the rep to talk about the kinds of questions the customer is asking, which will vary depending on their step of buying. The customer could be wondering whether their need is big enough to invest in a change at this time, given other priorities. Or they may be far enough along to be thinking about specific capabilities they want to see, or they may be interested in knowing how your solution compares to your number one competitor's. And not to sound too cynical, but don't take the rep's word for it when they give you an answer! Ask them *how* they know what step of buying the customer is in. Probe into those exit criteria!

2. **What problem is the customer trying to solve?** Another trap that reps fall into is spending so much time discussing the features and benefits of your solution that they forget to think about what it is a solution to! That is, what is the problem that the customer is trying to solve? Keeping reps focused on customer problems is critical for value-based selling.

3. **Which decision makers will be on the call, and where are they in the buying process?** Here's another challenge with focus that sales reps often have. They have probably talked primarily with one person in the client or prospect company— but maybe there will be others on the call. A rep needs to anticipate who will be on the call (or at the meeting) and what those decision makers' needs and priorities are.

Of course, you want to end every conversation by asking what specific steps the rep wants the customer to take after the call or meeting. That is, what go-forward action commitment are they looking for?

2. "What's happening with . . . ?"

Probably one of the most common conversations a manager has with a rep starts with "what's happening with . . . ?" or perhaps "what are you going to sell?" The real aim of this conversation is to talk about what needs to happen, or what steps the rep has to take to move the deal toward closing. How this kind of conversation goes is very different depending on whether you have a typical sales process vs. a buying-focused process.

Let's look at an example: The scenario is that a sales rep is selling software that provides enterprise users the ability to share files, while maintaining security, from any device, including smartphones. The rep's prospect is a large law firm with whom several initial conversations have already taken place. The manager wants a status report.

In a company with a traditional sales process (like Company Alpha in Chapter 5):

> *Manager: Where are we at with the Sunsational Law Firm deal?*
>
> Rep: It's looking pretty good. I've got a good rapport with the key decision maker, and I hope to schedule a demo for next week. It should close by the end of next month.
>
> *Manager: Any potential landmines you know of?*
>
> Rep: Nope. My contact has responded quickly to all my requests, so I think we're in good shape.
>
> *Manager: OK, great. Keep me posted.*

In a company with a buying-focused funnel (like Company Beta in Chapter 5):

> *Manager: Our funnel shows that Sunsational Law Firm is beginning to grapple with the discontent they have with their current software. Are they still at that stage of buying? And what makes you think they are or aren't moving forward?*
>
> Rep: They're moving into their Research phase. I met last week with their administrator and she discussed

her concerns about unsecure file sharing. In the past, the firm has relied on a manual process of saving confidential files to a flash drive and shipping overnight via courier service. But recently she's become aware that some partners have been sharing files via unsecure consumer platforms.

Manager: Did your prospect talk about the economic implications and costs of their problems?

Rep: Yes. She says the firm is spending upwards of $500 per day on courier services. And she's concerned about the potential liability of the unsecure file transfers.

Manager: What could happen now that might send this deal sideways?

Rep: Well, she hasn't really involved other decision makers yet, which I know will be critical in making the final decision.

Manager: I think you could try asking her questions that she doesn't know the answer to—questions that only other decision makers can answer. That should get her to involve other decision makers. When is your next meeting scheduled and what customer action objective have you set for that meeting?

Rep: My plan in the next meeting is to identify her buying criteria and suggest a few additional issues that she should be thinking about that link to our competitive strengths. Your suggestion about the questions is great. I think I could draft up some more questions that either their tech guy or lead partner would need to answer. Then I can aim at getting her to agree to schedule a technical deep-dive with her and the project team next week.

3. Is your rep ready for a presentation?

Have a suspicion that a sales rep isn't fully prepared for an important sales presentation? Concerned they may end up looking like a deer in the headlights when prospects start raising questions? Well before the presentation, ask the rep the following customer- and buying-focused questions:

1. What is your understanding of the customer's buying criteria?

2. Which of these represent a competitive edge for us? Which of these represent a competitive disadvantage for us?

3. Who is positioned most favorably at this time, you or a competitor?

4. What can you do to influence the customer's criteria so that they see a better match between their needs and our offering?

5. What are three reasons this customer should buy from us? (Listen for a connection between each of your company's strengths and an explicit customer need.)

If the rep cannot answer one or more of these questions satisfactorily, walk them through the actions they need to take (and the prospect needs to take) to get the answers.

Improving Your One-on-One Monthly Reviews

In earlier chapters, I made a point of saying that typical one-on-one monthly reviews often do little to help develop sales reps' skills. That's because most sales managers rely on reviewing the sales results to spot problems.

Regularly scheduled one-on-ones are a critical part of sales management because they help both you and your reps keep track of their behaviors and activities, important sales opportunities, forecasts, and strategies to succeed. The goal I am championing in this book includes repurposing one-on-one monthly reviews to become more of a developmental coaching conversation, where the rep and manager conclude the meeting with clearly defined strategies for improvement as well as a shared understanding of the current status of deals in the works.

A common mistake many managers make is focusing this conversation only on the opportunities expected to close this month and ignoring new opportunities created.

Without a doubt, putting new opportunities into the funnel is one of the most challenging parts of the sales profession. For most sellers, it's the least desirable part of the job. And since most salespeople work without supervision, this regular one-on-one is essential for ensuring that your salespeople are continuing to do what is expected of them.

If you don't discuss new opportunities, then many salespeople won't put them into your CRM system until much later in the sales cycle. They do this to avoid having to answer your questions about those opportunities, but your forecasts will be much more accurate if you know about *all* deals that a rep is working on. So for that reason alone, you need to pay attention to new opportunities.

Also, if you don't discuss new opportunities with your salespeople on a monthly basis, reps can become complacent. The best way to defeat complacency is to prevent it. A monthly review discussion causes the salesperson to confront their own complacency before it leads to lower sales results.

As you might expect, however, I advise tweaking the typical format of such reviews so that it reinforces your buying-focused sales process. You'll see an example of how to do this in Figure 24, which is a preparation form that I give to managers to hand out to their salespeople (the rep fills out the form then brings it to the review meeting with the manager). The top half is probably similar to the topics you already discuss in these reviews, but note the "most recent customer action" column in the bottom half—that question ties directly to the exit criteria, which are defined based on what your customers are doing.

During this meeting you also want to discuss those opportunities where nothing has happened for 30 to 60 days. Probe the salesperson for their interpretations of why these deals have stopped progressing.

The one-on-one review meeting is a great time to do some sales opportunity coaching, too. Select one of the deals the rep is forecasting to close and ask the coaching questions listed in Figure 23 (p. 183). The five questions listed on page 188 may also be helpful to ask, too. The rep's answers should provide you with valuable insight on the likelihood that the deal being discussed will close as forecasted and, if not, why not. Then, put a two-pronged plan in place: Coach the rep on how to get the deal back on track and set up a coaching plan to help the rep do better the next time.

Using one-on-ones to improve yourself!

I once asked my sales team to respond to a confidential survey and was surprised by what I learned. Prior to the survey, I had a mindset that the last thing I wanted to do was micromanage. But from the survey I learned that my team interpreted my reluctance to get involved as an unwillingness to coach them. The feedback wasn't easy to hear, but it was critical in helping me become a more effective coach—and improving my team's results!

This lesson was reinforced when I read Samuel Culbert's great book, *Get Rid of the Performance Review!*[29] Culbert suggests that managers ask their employees three questions:

1. What are you getting from me that you like and find helpful?
2. What are you getting from me that limits your effectiveness?
3. What are you *not* getting from me that would help you produce more? Why do you think that would help you at this time?

I think all sales managers should ask these questions at the end of the monthly reviews, or any other regular conversation they have with a rep. It's not always easy to hear the responses, but I guarantee you'll gain insights that will help you become a more effective manager and coach.

---

29 Samuel Culbert (with Lawrence Rout), *Get Rid of the Performance Review!: How Companies Can Stop Intimidating, Start Managing—and Focus on What Really Matters* (Business Plus, 2010).

Figure 24: Monthly Review Discussion Form

Monthly 1-on-1

Results

Discuss year-to-date, previous quarter, and previous month results. Share the rep's ranking on the team.

Funnel Review

New opportunities added since last review & potential revenue:

Existing opportunities that have moved forward since our previous discussion:

Opportunities forecasted to close vs. plan

Customer	Most recent customer action	Why we'll win	Potential revenue	Probability of success

Agreed-upon next steps:

What Happens When a Deal Is Lost?

Nobody, no matter how good they are at selling, has a 100 percent win rate. That means all of us have to learn how to deal with losses. Since having a positive attitude is particularly important in the sales profession, it can be very harmful if a salesperson gets too discouraged after a loss. That's a normal human reaction, but staying down is not good. I've seen it happen; you likely have too.

So part of your "coaching for the win" repertoire has to be how to help sales reps learn and quickly recover from lost sales. A lost sale is a failure only when we, individually and as a team, don't learn from it, or if we allow it to harm the rep's ability to work on new and existing opportunities.

One of the simplest ways to do this is to have the rep take notes on what they learned from each deal (whether they win or lose). I've seen this method work in a variety of situations. My wife, for example, is working hard on her golf game, with a goal to break 100. Every time she goes out golfing, she carries a little notebook in her golf bag. At the end of the round she writes down what she learned. And you know what? She finally shot a 99. Hurray!

Another way to help people learn is to share your experiences with similar situations when you were a rep. What went wrong in your situation? What did you learn to do differently because of it?

As the sales manager, it is also your responsibility to lead the post-mortem on all major lost deals because your rep is not going to ask the customer questions that may reflect poorly on their own sales efforts. The rep is probably dejected about losing the sale and may not be thinking clearly. Therefore, you need to step up and ask the customer probing questions that your salesperson wouldn't ask.

Immediately upon learning that a major sales opportunity has been lost, contact the customer and say, "Thanks for letting us know. We're not going to try and change your mind. But we would like to ask you a few questions so we can get better." Have your salesperson join you on the call, but you take the lead and ask the customer these questions:

- What did they (the winning company) do that were positive reasons why you chose their solution?

- How did we compare, in your eyes, on these important priorities?

- Which aspect of your needs do you feel we didn't understand as well as the company you selected?

- What one or two recommendations do you have for us that would help us get better?

- Will we have a chance to win your business again in the future?

Great sales managers learn from losses. From a coaching and leadership standpoint, the reasons why your rep lost and the customer's recommendations for improvement need to be shared immediately with all members of your team. That's how your team becomes more competitive.

Getting in Sync With Buying and Selling

The underlying theme of this chapter is captured in the motto I use all the time that I referenced earlier: "Slow down." It's a phrase that is meant to remind reps that they need to slow down their selling so they can stay in sync with customer buying behavior. It's also a phrase I'm starting to use with sales managers as a way to help them get in sync with their reps throughout the selling process, not just at the end.

When you reinforce a buying focus with your reps by asking them customer-focused questions, you get them to look at a purchase from the customer's buying perspective. They, in turn, will start to ask more targeted questions of your customers. What they learn by asking those questions will help them become sensitive to the twists and turns that send deals off track. They will gain a greater understanding of customers' problems and needs—better than that of your competitors' reps—which will allow them to improve their selling process. Their insights will better prepare them to resolve the challenges that both you and the customer face at each step along the way. That's how you can help your customers move more quickly through their buying process. And that's why if your salespeople slow down, they will sell faster!

From your perspective as a manager, I'm advising that you slow down to talk with reps about what they are and aren't learning from prospects and what steps those prospects are or aren't taking. That will put you in a much stronger position to provide timely guidance and advice that will help your salespeople secure more wins. And isn't that what we all want?

Section 4

Taking Action

Overview

The British philosopher Herbert Spencer once said, "The great aim of education is not knowledge, but action." My purpose in writing this book was to help sales leaders—whether managers or higher ups—realize the broad scope of topics that sales managers need to master to create a great sales team. Now it's time to consider the challenges faced by you and your team and set priorities for the specific actions that will help you drive consistent sales growth.

Going into the details of strategy development and implementation planning are beyond the scope of this book. However, I thought it imperative that I help you head off in the right direction.

So the single chapter in this section—**Chapter 10: Shape a Championship Strategy**—pulls together themes from throughout the book to provide a practical model you can use to create a development plan for yourself and your team. The model will guide you in identifying a stretch goal and the specific tactics to help you achieve that goal.

Chapter 10

Shape a Championship Strategy

David Epstein, author of *The Sports Gene*, has devoted much of his career to studying the behavior of elite athletes and champions. In an interview he gave in conjunction with one of his TED talks,[30] he discussed a pattern he noticed in how champions set their goals. The TED program had just had a segment about Diana Nyad, the first person to complete the swim from Cuba to the Florida Keys without a shark cage. (It was her fifth attempt and she was 64 years old.)

All of the champions he studied, said Epstein, have "Diana Nyad-sized feats off in the distance"—meaning major goals they want to accomplish, such as winning a race or an Olympic medal. But on a daily basis they aren't thinking about that end point. Rather, every day will be devoted to something very specific, such as "today in my workout, between mile three and four, I'm going to push hard." In other words, said Epstein, these champions are really good at setting proximate (near-term) objectives that tell them what to do today.

---

30 "Champions: David Epstein: Are Athletes Really Getting Faster, Better, Stronger?" TED Radio Hour, NPR, July 18, 2004, http://www.npr.org/programs/ted-radio-hour/331331360/champions

What I want to do in this chapter is show how these concepts of "Diana Nyad-sized feats" and "proximate objectives"—coupled with some essential planning skills—can work to help you create a championship sales team.

Setting a Breakthrough Goal

Many sales managers set modest or uninspiring goals because they don't want to overpromise and then come up short. But you can't play it safe if you want to truly inspire your team. The journey to realizing a championship sales team has to start with having a breakthrough or stretch goal—by which I mean a level of performance your team has never achieved before, something currently beyond its capability (or so everyone thinks!), something the equivalent of swimming from Cuba to Florida or winning an Olympic gold medal. Those are the goals that will shape the plans you develop and implement.

As Michelangelo said, "The greater danger for most of us isn't that our aim is too high and we miss it, but that it is too low and we reach it."

Suppose, for example, that your quota is to increase sales by 15 percent this year over last year. You need to set a breakthrough goal higher than that. The higher goal covers the possibility that one of your salespeople will fall short or quit, so that the least you could do is meet the quota increase and ideally you could exceed it.

What's the worst that can happen? A year from now, maybe you won't have achieved the breakthrough goal—remember, it took Diana Nyad five attempts to achieve her breakthrough goal—but I guarantee that you will have gone further than you previously thought possible. You can celebrate your success and then set another stretch goal!

The next step is defining the intermediate targets—more actionable objectives—that collectively will put you in a better position to accomplish the breakthrough goal.

Focus and Urgency

The best way to improve your team's results is to improve yourself and your team. The previous chapters of this book have, I hope, given you a lot of ideas that can help you improve as a manager and increase your team's sales. And if we were all superhuman, we could work on all of these things at once. Knowing that's not possible, it's up to you to decide which improvement initiatives to focus on and how you can create a sense of urgency within your team for achieving the intermediate objective so you can ultimately reach the breakthrough goal.

The possibilities are endless, depending on what is most important to you and your team. Consider these examples:

- Are there sales instincts that prevent you from becoming a more effective leader?

- Is poor time management leaving you with little time to allocate to coaching?

- Are there poor attitudes or wills among sales reps that are demotivating your whole team?

- Does your team need more training and coaching on developing a buying-process focus?

- Is your forecasting a mess because reps aren't using your CRM system regularly or aren't entering opportunities as soon as they arise?

- Do you need to redefine your sales funnel (or sales process) to be more customer-focused?

- Do you need to do more early-cycle sales coaching to help reps get more deals in the funnel or secure bigger deals?

- Do you need to better triage your coaching time? Or work on developing your coaching skills so you become more of a teacher and less of a critic?

- Do you need to recommit to monthly one-on-one review discussions that also cover new sales opportunities?

Of course, this list is just a few of the questions you may be thinking about. I'm sure your organization has specific guidance around planning and employee development that would make the list even longer.

In short, I'm sure you could easily come up with dozens of ideas for actionable objectives that would contribute to the accomplishment of your breakthrough goal. Trying to do too much can be just as bad as doing too little, however, so I always tell sales managers to pick a few priorities to focus on for planning. There's no way to quantify the potential impact of these alternatives, no way to determine ahead of time if working on your own mindset would be more valuable to the team than additional sales team training on customer buying, for example. So I'll leave it up to your judgment and experience to decide where you should focus first. Once those priorities are chosen, the time has come to turn dreams into actions.

Planning: Turning Dreams into Actions

As mundane as it may sound, the secret to having a championship sales team often lies in whether you, the team's manager, have a written plan that connects the actionable objectives (which are tied to the breakthrough goal) to the implementation details that will shape daily decisions about your leadership priorities. That translation from the dream to specific actions is something that only you can do for your team. No one else can fill that role.

The necessity of a written plan

Plans for creating a champion team can't just be in your head. You need to write them down.

Why? We all encounter issues every day that take us away from our priorities. A written plan helps us fight that battle by constantly reminding us of what is truly *important* and not just *urgent*. It's a magnet that keeps you connected to your priorities in a way that sales managers without a plan cannot be.

If you don't have a written plan, then all of your ideas become jumbled in your head and you will have a harder time sticking to priorities and communicating those priorities to your team. That uncertainty causes you unnecessary stress.

While every company has its own standards around what a plan should look like, in my experience there are five essential components that have to be included or else you will struggle with implementation:

1. Actionable objective tied to the breakthrough goal

2. Current situation

3. Resistance and roadblocks

4. Action steps

5. Resources

To help sales managers organize their thoughts on these five elements, I have them capture their thoughts on a form like that shown in Figure 25.

Figure 25

Objective #1	
Name a specific, measurable objective you want to achieve in three to six months.	
	Link to breakthrough goal: · Deadline:

Current situation	
Where are you now? Be brutally honest.	

Roadblocks	
What obstacles stand in your way? Why aren't you currently able to achieve this objective?	

Actions needed

	Describe the step	Start date	End date
1			
2			
3			
4			
5			

List the actions in sequence that you will need to take to achieve the objective and overcome obstacles.

Resources required

What people, funding, support, etc., do you need to complete the actions on time?

Here is a brief description of each planning step, followed by excerpts from a completed plan.

1. Actionable objective

Describe the actionable objective, the intermediate target that will get you closer to the breakthrough goal. It's important that you focus on a limited number—say, two to five objectives—that you think will propel you and your team the closest to the breakthrough goal.

While these objectives can be anything, I insist that one of them be linked to team development (for all the reasons I've spelled out earlier in this book).

2. Current situation

You need to be brutally honest about where your team is at right now and what is going on. And I do mean brutally honest—any planning based on an inaccurate or incomplete understanding of the current state is fundamentally flawed.

Typically, the description will focus on the current **performance level of your team and individual reps**. For example, where are your reps in terms of skill and will? What percentage of the quota do they regularly achieve? Overall, what are the biggest strengths you see on your team and the biggest weaknesses? Are there any Bell Cows? Prima donnas? Bad apples whose poor attitudes are infectious?

If you're going to include your own leadership development objectives on the plan, since your attitudes and skills affect the whole team, then you have to be honest about your current situation, as well. List the sales instincts you fall prey to or where you're lacking in leadership skills.

3. Resistance and roadblocks

We all know the old saying that you can't get different results by simply repeating the same actions over and over again. If you want your team's future to be different, you will need to change something in how you work with your team. This could include any of the following:

- Setting new expectations about attitudes and behaviors (the importance of wills)

- Developing a new focus on buying behavior (which reps may not be aware of)

- Spending more time one-on-one with reps (which they may see as a loss of independence)

- Expecting reps to solve more of their own problems

- Reacting sooner to poor performance

Any one of these changes could potentially raise resistance, and it's likely you'll be doing most or all of them!

In addition to this potential resistance, other factors could make it harder for your team to achieve its goals, such as these examples:

- **Product/service line changes or challenges.** Is your company about to launch new offerings? Retire old offerings? Try to expand into new territories or markets? What are your competitors doing that may change the market landscape?

- **Organizational changes or challenges.** Is there anything going on in your company that may affect your team's ability to achieve a certain goal? A merger, an acquisition, IT changes, a move, consolidation, reorganization, changes in the compensation plan?

Alan Lakein, the author of several now-classic books on time management,[31] said, "Planning is bringing the future into the present so that you can do something about it now." Project yourself a year into the future and think about the most likely reasons you'd use to explain why your team *didn't* achieve its breakthrough goal. Was it resistance? Market or product changes? Organizational changes? Pick one or at most a few factors that might be at work and include in your planning ideas for how to lower the resistance or deal with the obstacle.

4. Action steps

List the action steps needed to ensure you and your team can achieve your objective (and eventually the breakthrough goal). Depending on the objective, these action steps could include a wide range of activities for you and your team. Here are several examples:

- **Team development priorities and how you'll make that happen:** Are there low skill ratings that could be improved by training? When and how will that happen? What about low will ratings that require more direct attention from you? How and when will you deal with that?

- **Connections you need to make with other departments or leaders:** How do you build a stronger relationship with marketing so your team gets better quality leads?

- **Forecasting and opportunity development:** Do you need to coach the earlier stages of sales opportunities so your reps can better qualify leads and you can improve forecast accuracy? Do you need to increase CRM usage?

---

31 For example, see Alan Lakein, *How to Get Control of Your Time and Your Life* (Signet, 1989).

- **Hiring and de-hiring:** Is it time to let a poor performer go? Do you need to hire someone? What will it take to make these things happen?

5. Resources

What people, funding, or support do you need that is different from what you have now? Do you need a better incentive reward when a salesperson achieves their breakthrough number? Team recognition event? Training? Define the resources that you will need, and communicate that to your boss.

Tying the Components Together

To show how all of the plan components come together, I've compiled an example you'll see in Figure 26. The scenario is that the manager has set a breakthrough goal of increasing sales by 25 percent this year over last year, with a breakthrough team development goal of increasing skill and will ratings by 20 percent in one year. She has set several targets to achieve in the first six months, one around quotas and two around team development (closing skill gaps and removing demotivators).

Figure 26

	Production	Team Development
Actionable Objective	• Improve win rate on forecasted deals to 60%.	• Close skill gaps and remove demotivators.
Link to breakthrough goal	• Need to reach 65% to achieve a +25% gain in sales.	• These actions should raise both skill and will ratings and can be accomplished quickly.

	Production	Team Development
Current situation	• As a whole, the team achieved 89% of its sales quota the past year. • Only two out of eight reps achieved their annual plan last year; one of them is the team Bell Cow who is currently at 125% of plan YTD and recently won a President's Club award. • Only 52% of deals forecasted to close were actually won. • Deal review meetings are ad hoc and inconsistent and no lessons carry over.	• Average skill rating across team: 3.2 out of 5. • Average will rating: 3.5 out of 5 and declining. • Two new salespeople hired within past six months.
Roadblocks	• Lack of project management resources. • Sales team is lacking in process discipline. • Sales manager (me) not driving deal reviews.	• Senior rep has a negative attitude and is infecting team morale. His numbers are also declining. (He has become a bad apple.) • Getting new people up to speed quickly.
Tactics/ actions	• Increase time spent on process coaching (improve buy awareness and discipline to our process) • Complete all postmortems on $50k+ deals lost within 3 days of notification. Share learnings and add to best practices. • Get with Ops Team leadership to gather info on how to improve our implementation plans.	• Confront bad apple. Manage up, or out, by April 1st. • Get with HR to initiate hiring process to replace bad apple. • Increase time spent coaching salespeople to 12 hours per week. • Spend time with new hires now! Establish a mentor relationship between my Bell Cow and two new-hires.
Resources needed	• Get budget for more team challenges and promo events	• None

As you can see in the figure, this manager could end up with just two pages (using the goals worksheet shown on p. 206) that capture all of the key information regarding her goals and plan. She can then use these two pages as guideposts for the next six months, quickly reviewing them every day to help her remember priorities and tactics. This kind of brief summary is often more useful than having more elaborate plans.

Measuring Progress

I don't think anyone imagines for an instant that the first time a champion measures performance is when they are competing. Far from it. They use data to help them understand where they are now, how far they've come, and how much further they have to progress to achieve their breakthrough goal.

For a sales manager, this data should include the metrics listed below at a minimum (you will likely have additional metrics related to your goals). Note that the first one—percent of plan—is the only end result or outcome. As I discussed earlier in the book, knowing results is essential in our profession, but we need to guard against becoming *solely* focused on outcomes because it makes us short-sighted; we can more easily slide back into the habit of chasing big deals instead of spending our time coaching so that our *salespeople* can win even more big deals. To balance the picture, the other metrics in this set are process or input metrics. They reflect how well you're managing the inputs that produce the results.

1) Percent of plan; number of reps "on plan"

This first metric is one that all sales managers are familiar with: Percent of plan reflects where your team is compared to the annual goal or plan, usually expressed as what percentage of the sales targets your team has achieved.

What you also should be tracking, however, is the **number (or**

percentage) of reps who are "on plan" (their sales numbers are right on target for the quarter or year). This metric ensures that you stay focused on improving your entire team, not just the good performers or bad performers. Your reps will get the message that all of them matter to the team, which improves morale. And the better you do on this metric, the better your overall team health.

2) New hire productivity

This measures how quickly you ramp up new hires. Define what results you expect of new hires over their first year on the job. For example, set sales targets in the three quarters following their first quarter (months 4–6, months 7–9, and months 10–12). Then measure your new hires on what percentage of those targets they achieved. (Ideally, you would be able to get data from other sales managers as well so you could gauge yourself against the norms in your company.) Use this data as a reminder to provide the necessary time and attention to new hires to ensure they ramp up to quota quickly, and look for an improvement in the percentage over time.

3) Skill and will ratings

This category is here to make sure that you stay focused on the developmental needs of your team. If you follow my recommendations in Chapter 3, you should be doing skill and will ratings on your team at least annually, and preferably biannually or even quarterly. You could calculate the overall rating for your team on both metrics.

As an example, Table K shows the ratings for the sales team I discussed in Chapter 6, along with the average score for both categories. I used a scale of 1 to 5 for these ratings; you may want to use a different scale. As I described in that chapter, Willy Sellmore repeatedly failed to improve and I eventually had to de-hire him. Then I hired Ivan Inkling, someone who was unskilled but very enthusiastic. You can see the improvement in the team's will ratings were immediate (Table L). Plus, I knew that Ivan would quickly improve his skills because of his "humble and hungry" attitude, so my target was to get the team's average skill rating up to at least a 4 as well.

Table K: Skill and Will Ratings (original)

Name	Skill	Will
Ann T. Oxidant	5	5
Clare Voyant	2	3
Sal Monella	3	5
Willy Sellmore	2	2
Carlotta Tendant	5	2
Al Fresco	4	4
Average	3.5	3.5

Table L: Skill and Will Ratings (with new hire Ivan Inkling)

Name	Skill	Will
Ann T. Oxidant	5	5
Clare Voyant	2	3
Sal Monella	3	5
Ivan Inkling	**2**	**5**
Carlotta Tendant	5	2
Al Fresco	4	4
Average	3.5	4

Comparing multiple teams

If you're an executive in charge of overseeing multiple teams, I recommend you monitor each team using the metrics described in this chapter, and track two additional measures:

- **Number of reps promoted.** Any business that wants to grow must focus on growing its future leaders. Perhaps there is no more important metric than this one, because it tells you how effective your sales managers are at (a) hiring and (b) developing those people to such a high level that they are chosen for promotion into a sales management position.

- **Turnover/retention.** Some turnover is good. Too much turnover can be devastating. You don't want zero turnover because that would indicate that your sales managers are hanging on to poor performers too long. But on the flipside, too much turnover—and especially the loss of successful salespeople—can be devastating to a team. **The number one reason why productive salespeople leave an organization is their relationship with their immediate supervisor.** This metric can help you evaluate how effective your managers are at creating a sales culture that experienced salespeople want to be a part of, as well as one that weeds out the rotten apples.

The Three Questions that Matter Most

My goal in writing *The Sales Manager's Guide to Greatness* has been to offer a range of proven strategies and practical tips on how to apply them. Knowing that the possibilities for improvement can seem endless and confusing, the advice on goal setting and the planning tool covered in this chapter were aimed at helping you navigate through the maze and simplify what you want to accomplish in the near future.

The theme of simplicity was driven home to me years ago when my first employer, Lanier Worldwide, hired Lou Holtz (the legendary college football coach) to come speak to our group of 100 sales managers.

Holtz told us that coaching a football team and coaching a sales team have a lot in common. He said that in football it's real easy to overcomplicate things with a massively thick playbook packed with Xs and Os. But at the end of the day, according to Holtz, your team members ask three fundamental questions of you:

1. Do you know what you are talking about?

2. Can I trust you?

3. Do you care about me?

I'm confident that each and every person who reads this book will have teams who answer "yes!" to each of Holtz's questions. That means that your heart is in the right place. Now, make sure that your actions support your intent. Pull the ideas from this book that are most meaningful and relevant to the challenges you face—and build your champion team!

If you'd like to stay in touch, visit our website at www.topline leadership.com where I blog on how-to tips for sales leaders and other sales leadership topics. I wish you much success!

Index

About Kevin F. Davis

Kevin F. Davis is the president of TopLine Leadership Inc., a leading provider of customizable sales and sales management training programs targeted at helping clients drive consistent sales growth.

Kevin has more than 30 years of experience, having worked his way up from sales rep, to sales manager, to general manager. He therefore understands the particular challenges faced when transitioning into management and when transitioning to managing managers. Kevin continues to draw on his firsthand experiences to help his clients remove barriers in the way of great success.

Under Kevin's guidance, TopLine helps sales managers organize their priorities—separate out the merely urgent from the truly important—to elevate overall performance and boost efficiency. Sales managers discover how to transition their coaching style from one that primarily judges lagging indicators to a more balanced approach that includes proactive developmental coaching.

TopLine's salesforce programs are focused on establishing a consistent, repeatable sales process and sales funnel linked to the buying process. This helps sales reps develop more effective sales strategies, be more effective in every customer meeting, and be more accurate in predicting deal closings.

Kevin is the author of two sales books: The first, *Getting Into Your Customer's Head: 8 Secret Roles of Selling Your Competitors Don't Know*, was selected as one of the top 30 business books of 1996 by Soundview Executive Book Summaries. The second, *Slow Down, Sell Faster! Understand Your Customer's Buying Process and Maximize Your Sales* breaks the entrenched myth that a faster sales pitch leads to a faster close.